Scott Foresman

Fluency

Teacher's Guide and Student Worktext

Glenview, Illinois
Boston, Massachusetts
Chandler, Arizona
Upper Saddle River, New Jersey

ISBN-13: 978-0-328-47747-0
ISBN-10: 0-328-47747-8
3 4 5 6 7 8 9 10 V084 18 17 16 15 14 13 12 11 10

Reading Street Response to Intervention Kit

Program Overview

The *Reading Street Response to Intervention Kit* provides targeted instruction in core English-Language Arts standards for Grades 3 to 6 in each of the five critical areas of reading instruction: phonemic awareness, phonics and decoding, fluency, vocabulary, and comprehension. The Kit, designed for small-group or one-on-one instruction, includes lessons on core skills, allowing teachers to focus on the skills students need most and to help them make rapid progress to achieve grade-level proficiency. For additional information about the *Reading Street Response to Intervention Kit,* see "How to Use This Kit" in the RTI Kit Implementation Guide.

Fluency Teacher's Guide and Student Worktext

The Teacher's Guide portion includes

- three-tiered, differentiated lessons
- specific guidance on how to measure fluency
- reinforcement for the strategies and routines used in the core program
- three customized mini-lessons differentiated for the following reading and skill levels:

  Odd-numbered lessons focus on these Words Correct Per Minute:
  - Mini-lesson 1: Level 1 (20–45 WCPM)
  - Mini-lesson 2: Level 2 (40–65 WCPM)
  - Mini-lesson 3: Level 3 (60–85 WCPM)

  Even-numbered lessons focus on these Words Correct Per Minute:
  - Mini-lesson 1: Level 1 (80–105 WCPM)
  - Mini-lesson 2: Level 2 (100–125 WCPM)
  - Mini-lesson 3: Level 3 (120–145 WCPM)

The Student Worktext portion includes

- additional reading opportunities
- additional skills practice
- School+Home activities on every page

Lesson Features

- **Set the scene** introduces the lesson topic to students.
- **Objectives** identify the instructional objectives for students.
- **Materials** list the Worktext components and additional supporting materials for the lesson, such as the Leveled Reader Database.
- **Direct teaching** is provided through explicit teacher modeling and consistent routines.
- **Mini-lessons** provide differentiated instruction.
- **Guided practice** for each mini-lesson consists of ample group practice with multiple response opportunities.
- **Independent practice (On Their Own)** allows students to read independently, with a partner, or with a small group.
- **If.../then...** provides teachers with specific activities for reinforcing skills.

Table of Contents
Fluency

Readability in *Reading Street Response to Intervention Kit*

Students' reading levels in a single classroom often range greatly. In the Fluency Teacher's Guide and Student Worktext, mini-lessons and the corresponding Worktext reading passages are differentiated to cover a range of reading levels.

Odd-numbered Lessons

Mini-lesson 1: Level 1 (20–45 WCPM)

The Worktext reading passages have a readability index of 1.5 to 1.9. Passages range from 65 to 115 words.

Mini-lesson 2: Level 2 (40–65 WCPM)

The Worktext reading passages have a readability index of 1.5 to 3.9 and range from 85 to 145 words.

Mini-lesson 3: Level 3 (60–85 WCPM)

Reading passages have a readability index of 4.0 to 5.0 and range from 140 to 180 words.

Even-numbered Lessons

Mini-lesson 1: Level 1 (80–105 WCPM)

The Worktext reading passages have a readability index of 1.5 to 1.9 and range from 165 to 200 words.

Mini-lesson 2: Level 2 (100–125 WCPM)

The Worktext reading passages have a readability index of 1.5 to 3.9. Passages range from 185 to 225 words.

Mini-lesson 3: Level 3 (120–145 WCPM)

Reading passages have a readability index of 4.0 to 5.0 and range from 240 to 275 words.

How to Measure Fluency

Use this routine with students when they are capable of doing timed self-assessments. Remind students that good readers read without mistake, with expression, and at a natural speed–as if they are speaking. Emphasize that learning to read this way takes practice and that keeping track of reading times helps students see how their reading improves with practice.

1. Introduce Timed Reading

Tell students that today they will read a story, such as "Look Both Ways" on Worktext p. 8, and keep track of how many words they read correctly in one minute. Explain that the numbers on the right side of the story are a running total of the words in the story.

Tell students that you will set a timer for one minute. They will underline any words they don't know as they read. When the timer goes off, students will draw a line after the last word they read.

2. Complete the First Timed Reading

Emphasize to students that timing their reading is not a race. The most important thing is to understand what they read. Encourage students to read the best they can. Tell students that they will start reading when you say "Begin."

Choose a passage that is neither too short nor too long, such as "Look Both Ways" on Worktext p. 8. Set the timer for one minute and have students whisper read the passage, marking it as you've instructed. Provide encouragement and prompting as needed.

3. Do the Numbers

After one minute, tell students that it's time to figure out how many words they read correctly. Show them how to use the words at the right of the story to identify the total number of words they read. Then have them count the words they underlined.

To figure out how many words they read correctly, tell students to take the total number of words they read and subtract the number of underlined words. For example, if their total is 85 words, and they underlined 5 words, they will subtract 5 from 85. That would mean they read 80 words correct per minute (80 WCPM).

4. Track Progress

Distribute the Fluency Progress Chart from p. T•9. Tell students that they will use the chart to keep track of how many words they read correctly in one minute. Explain that the numbers on the left show the number of words they read correctly. The numbers on the bottom show how many times the students checked their reading. When students check their reading the first time, they will fill in the column that has a 1 at the bottom.

For example, if students read 80 words right, they will find the number 80 in the very first column and draw a line. Then they will color in everything in that column under that line. Use a colored pencil to demonstrate. Help students calculate and chart the number of words they read correctly for the first timed reading.

5. Practice On Their Own

Before pairing students for practice, review each student's underlined words. Point out familiar sound-spellings or word parts to help students read the words, or identify unfamiliar words and their meanings for them.

Explain to students that they will read the passage several times, and then they will do another timed reading to find out how much their reading has improved. Work with students to set new WCPM goals for the second timed reading. Use goals that correspond to each student's grade-level goals.

Then pair students for practice. Have them take turns reading the story to each other three or four times. Tell partners to help each other with word identification and to encourage one another to read with expression.

6. Complete the Second Timed Reading

After sufficient practice, repeat the one-minute timed reading with the same passage. Have partners work together to figure out their words correct per minute (WCPM) and fill in their charts for their second timed reading. Have them determine if they reached the goal they set.

Name ____________________

Fluency Progress Chart

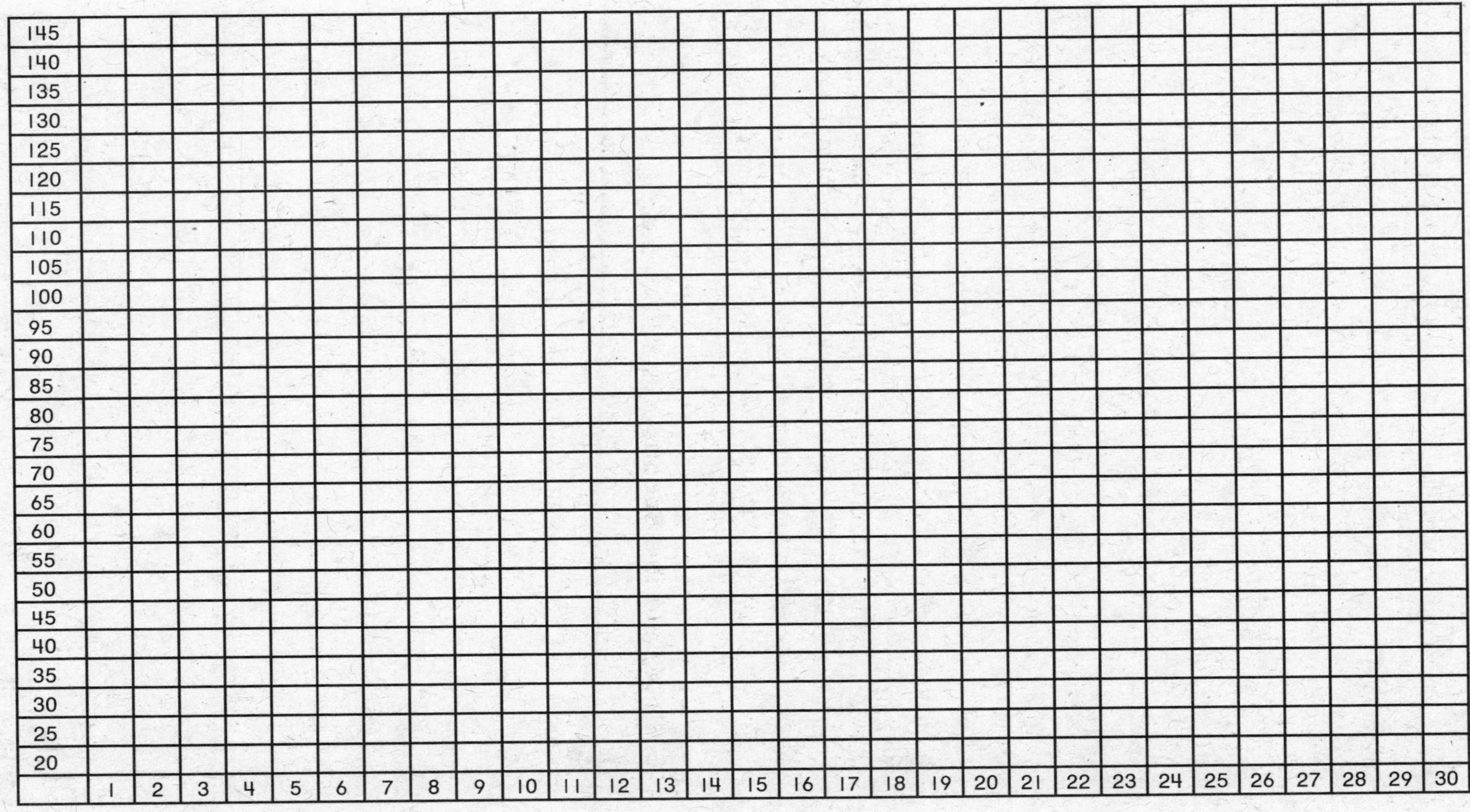

Fluency Teacher's Guide

Fluency Lesson 1

Accuracy 1

Objectives:

- Read fluently without errors, making sure to read each word correctly.

MATERIALS

Worktext pp. 2–7
Routine Cards 2, 8
Leveled Reader Database

Set the scene Introduce accuracy to students. Explain that in this lesson they will practice skills to make them better readers. Tell students they will practice reading without mistakes. They will read all the words correctly and not skip over or change any words. The more we practice reading, the better we get.

Model and teach Introduce the passage on Worktext p. 2. Today we'll read a story called "Up All Night." When we finish reading the story, I will ask you a question.

Review periods with students. Many sentences end with a period. When we see a period, we should pause before beginning to read the next sentence.

- Tell students that you will now read the first two sentences aloud. Tell them that you want to read every word accurately. I want to read without skipping over words or changing words. Point out periods at the end of each sentence. If there is a period at the end of a sentence, I will pause before reading the next sentence.
- Tell students that they will be able to read passages more easily if they are familiar with the words. One way to learn new words is to read the passage silently first. Pause to model reading silently.

Have students follow along as you model reading the first two sentences with no mistakes. Model pausing at the end of each sentence.

Check comprehension What does Adrian want for his birthday? (Adrian wants to stay up all night.)

Fluency Goal: 20–45 words correct per minute

Remind students that…

- they should read every word in the passage without skipping any.
- mispronouncing or misidentifying words can change their meaning.
- a period at the end of a sentence indicates that students should pause in their reading.

Guide Practice

Continue modeling accuracy by reading the next four sentences of "Up All Night" on Worktext p. 2. As you read, skip or mispronounce words, and ask students if they had trouble understanding your reading. Then model the sentences with no mistakes.

Give students time to read the passage silently before reading aloud with you.

If… students cannot read a word,

then… have them blend decodable words **(Routine Card 2)** or say and spell high-frequency words **(Routine Card 8)**.

On Their Own Prepare the group for a choral reading of "Up All Night." You are going to read the story aloud as a group. Remember to read every word. Try to read all the words correctly. When you see a period, pause for a moment.

Routine	Choral Reading
1. Read Together	Have students read aloud with you.
2. Reread	Then have students read aloud without you. For optimal fluency, students should reread three to four times.
3. Provide Feedback	Listen to students read and provide corrective feedback.

For additional practice, use "Melissa's New Room" on Worktext p. 3.

Mini-Lesson 2

Fluency Goal: 40–65 words correct per minute

Remind students that...

- they should read every word accurately and not skip over words.
- commas require a brief pause and end marks require a longer pause.
- a sentence sometimes continues onto the next line.

Guide Practice

Introduce the story "Canada" on Worktext p. 4. Review commas with students. When you see a comma, pause briefly. Then write the following words: *provinces, territories, prairies,* and *tundra.* Point to each word as you read it aloud. Then have students read the words with you and without you. Read aloud "Canada" with students. Make sure that they do not pause at the end of lines.

If... students have trouble pausing for periods,
then... model reading two sentences, pausing for the periods, and have students echo three or four times.

On Their Own Pair students to do an oral reading of "Canada."

Routine	Paired Reading
1. Reader 1 Begins	Reader 1 reads the story to Reader 2.
2. Reader 2 Begins	Reader 2 reads the story to Reader 1.
3. Reread	For optimal fluency, students should reread three to four times.
4. Provide Feedback	Listen to students read and provide corrective feedback.

Provide additional practice by having students read "Penguins" on Worktext p. 5 with a partner.

Mini-Lesson 3

Fluency Goal: 60–85 words correct per minute

Remind students that...

- they should read every word accurately.
- reading the story silently first will help them become familiar with the words.
- skipping or substituting words can change the meaning of a sentence.

Guide Practice

Introduce the story "Dad's Train" on Worktext p. 6. Remind students that reading sentences silently will help them become familiar with the words. Tell them to read the first paragraph silently.

Then ask students to read the first paragraph aloud with you. Model reading accurately.

If... students skip a word,
then... have them track selected text until they read it accurately. If they substitute a word, point to the word, sound it out, and read it correctly. Then model the sentence and have students repeat it.

On Their Own Pair students to do an oral reading of "Dad's Train."

Routine	Paired Reading
1. Reader 1 Begins	Reader 1 reads the story to Reader 2.
2. Reader 2 Begins	Reader 2 reads the story to Reader 1.
3. Reread	For optimal fluency, students should reread three to four times.
4. Provide Feedback	Listen to students read and provide corrective feedback regarding their fluency and their decoding.

For additional practice, use "Best Friends" on Worktext p. 7.

Fluency Lesson 2

Accuracy 2

Objectives:

- Read fluently without errors, making sure to read each word correctly.

MATERIALS

Worktext pp. 8–13
Routine Cards 2, 8
Leveled Reader Database

Set the scene Review accuracy with students. Explain that in today's lesson they will practice reading without making any mistakes. We will read all the words correctly and not skip over or substitute any words. Remember, the more you practice reading the passage, the better you will get.

Model and teach Introduce the passage on Worktext p. 8. Today we'll read a story called "Look Both Ways." When we finish reading the story, I will ask you a question.

Tell students that accuracy means reading every word correctly and not skipping words. If students read a word that they do not know, give them strategies to decode these words. They can look for familiar root words or affixes or break compound words into smaller words. They can also look up words in the dictionary. Learning new words will improve their reading and make reading more fun.

- Tell students that you will read the first two paragraphs aloud. I want to read without skipping over words or reading a word incorrectly.
- Suggest that students read each paragraph silently before they read it aloud. This will help them become familiar with the words. Model by reading silently to yourself.

Have students follow along as you model reading the first two paragraphs. First, provide a poor model by skipping, mispronouncing, or substituting some words. Then read accurately. Ask students which reading was easier to understand or more enjoyable. Discuss the differences.

Check comprehension Why does Sandy need to look both ways? (Sandy is crossing a busy street with cars on it.)

Fluency Goal: 80–105 words correct per minute

Remind students that…

- they should read every word without skipping any.
- mispronouncing or substituting words will make their reading harder to understand.
- reading silently before reading aloud will help them become familiar with words.

Guide Practice

Continue modeling accuracy by reading with no mistakes the rest of "Look Both Ways" on Worktext p. 8. Correctly pronounce *careful* and *shivers*, pointing to each word as you read it. Then prepare students to read aloud the story with you.

Give students time to read every two paragraphs silently before reading them aloud with you. Then read aloud with students, paying attention to accuracy.

If… students cannot read a word,
then… have them blend decodable words **(Routine Card 2)**.

On Their Own Prepare the group for a choral reading of "Look Both Ways."

Routine	Choral Reading
1. Read Together	Have students read aloud with you.
2. Reread	Then have students read aloud without you. For optimal fluency, students should reread three to four times.
3. Provide Feedback	Listen to students read and provide corrective feedback. Point out any words students skip over or read incorrectly.

If students read the passage fluently, provide additional practice by assigning "Election Day" on Worktext p. 9.

Mini-Lesson 2

Fluency Goal: 100–125 words correct per minute
Remind students that...

- they should read every word accurately.
- skipping words will change the meaning of a sentence.
- mispronouncing or substituting words makes the story difficult to understand.

Guide Practice
Introduce the story "The New Player" on Worktext p. 10. Point out the words in all capital letters. Explain to students that they should emphasize these words when they read. Model an accurate reading of the first two paragraphs.

Then give students time to read every two paragraphs silently before reading them aloud with you.

If... students are changing or omitting words,
then... model problematic sentences and have them track the print as they read. Work toward students reading without tracking.

On Their Own Pair students to do an oral reading of "The New Player."

Routine	Paired Reading
1. Reader 1 Begins	Reader 1 reads the story to Reader 2.
2. Reader 2 Begins	Reader 2 reads the story to Reader 1.
3. Reread	For optimal fluency, students should reread three to four times.
4. Provide Feedback	Listen to students read and provide corrective feedback. Point out any words students skip over or read incorrectly.

Provide additional practice by having students read "What the World Has to Offer" on Worktext p. 11 with a partner.

Mini-Lesson 3

Fluency Goal: 120–145 words correct per minute
Remind students that...

- they should read every word accurately.
- reading the story silently first will help them become familiar with the words.
- skipping or substituting words will change the meaning of the sentence.

Guide Practice
Introduce the story "A Day at Camp" on Worktext p. 12. Make sure students understand what a camp is. Read aloud the first two paragraphs and have students follow along.

Then have students read the next paragraph silently before reading it aloud with you. Repeat with the remaining paragraphs.

If... students skip or mispronounce a word,
then... point out the word, sound it out, and have children repeat it after you. Then read the whole sentence and have children repeat it.

On Their Own Pair students to do an oral reading of "A Day at Camp."

Routine	Paired Reading
1. Reader 1 Begins	Reader 1 reads the story to Reader 2.
2. Reader 2 Begins	Reader 2 reads the story to Reader 1.
3. Reread	For optimal fluency, students should reread three to four times.
4. Provide Feedback	Listen to students read and provide corrective feedback regarding their fluency and their decoding.

For additional practice, use "The Mystery of the Missing Balls" on Worktext p. 13.

Fluency Lesson 3
Rate 1

Objectives:
- Read fluently at a speed that sounds like natural speech.

MATERIALS
Worktext pp. 14–19
Routine Cards 2, 8
Leveled Reader Database

Set the scene Introduce the concept of rate. Today we're going to practice reading at a normal speed. If we read too fast or too slow, listeners have a hard time understanding the story. The best speed for us to use when reading is the same speed we use when talking.

Model and teach Introduce the passage on Worktext p. 14. Today we'll read a story called "The New Baby." Make sure students understand that a *hospital* is a place where doctors take care of people.

As students read longer passages, they will find that sentences do not always end at the end of each line. Remind students to pause for end marks. Otherwise, they should continue reading on the next line without pausing.

- Tell students that you will read the first paragraph aloud. I will be careful not to read too fast or too slow. I will read so that it sounds as if I'm talking to you.
- Remind students that becoming familiar with the words will help them read more smoothly. They can learn the words by reading silently before they read aloud. Pause to read to yourself.

Then have students follow along as you model reading the first paragraph. Read through the paragraph twice. In the first reading, read some sentences too fast and others too slow. In the second reading, pay special attention to reading at a normal rate. Ask students which reading they preferred and why. Discuss how reading at a natural rate makes the reading easier for listeners to understand.

Check comprehension Why is Kevin's mother in the hospital? (Kevin's mother had a baby.)

Fluency Goal: 20–45 words correct per minute
Remind students that...
- they should read as if they were talking to a friend.
- reading silently will help them become familiar with the words.
- reading too fast or too slow will make their reading difficult to understand.

Guide Practice
Model the concept of rate by reading the second paragraph of "The New Baby" on Worktext p. 14. Pay special attention to reading at an appropriate rate. Model tracking the text by pointing to each word as you read it aloud. Give students time to read the paragraph. Then read the second paragraph aloud with students.

If... students cannot read a word,

then... have them blend decodable words **(Routine Card 2)** or say and spell high-frequency words **(Routine Card 8)**.

On Their Own Prepare the group for a choral reading of "The New Baby." You are going to read the story aloud as a group. Remember to read every word. Try to read at the same speed that you normally speak.

Routine	**Choral Reading**
1. Read Together	Have students read aloud with you.
2. Reread	Then have students read aloud without you. For optimal fluency, students should reread three to four times.
3. Provide Feedback	Listen to students read and provide corrective feedback.

For additional practice, use "A New Trick" on Worktext p. 15.

Mini-Lesson 2

Fluency Goal: 40–65 words correct per minute

Remind students that...

- they should read at the same rate that they normally speak.
- commas require a brief pause.
- they should read neither too fast nor too slow.

Guide Practice

Introduce "Ryan Does Laundry" on Worktext p. 16. Remind students to pay attention to commas. There are commas between some words in the sentences. When you come to a comma, pause for a moment before continuing to read.

Model a fluent reading of the first paragraph. Then have students read the next paragraph silently before reading it aloud.

If... students are reading too quickly,
then... model reading a sentence and ask them to track the print to slow them down as they echo you. Model reading the sentence three or four times.

On Their Own Pair students to do an oral reading of "Ryan Does Laundry."

Routine	Paired Reading
1. Reader 1 Begins	Reader 1 reads the story to Reader 2.
2. Reader 2 Begins	Reader 2 reads the story to Reader 1.
3. Reread	For optimal fluency, students should reread three to four times.
4. Provide Feedback	Listen to students read and provide corrective feedback. Point out if students read too fast or too slow.

Provide additional practice by having students read "Piggy Banks" on Worktext p. 17 with a partner.

Mini-Lesson 3

Fluency Goal: 60–85 words correct per minute

Remind students that...

- they should read at a speed they recognize as the same as natural speech.
- reading silently before reading aloud will help them become familiar with words.
- they should read at a pace neither too fast nor too slow.

Guide Practice

Introduce the story "Growing Watermelons" on Worktext p. 18. Read aloud the first paragraph, reading too slowly. Then read again at a normal rate. Discuss the differences with students. Ask students to read the next paragraph silently. Then have them read it aloud with you.

If... students are reading too slowly,
then... model a sentence or a paragraph at a moderate rate and ask them to read it after you. Read three or four more times with students repeating, each time a bit faster, until students have achieved a normal rate.

On Their Own Pair students to do an oral reading of "Growing Watermelons."

Routine	Paired Reading
1. Reader 1 Begins	Reader 1 reads the story to Reader 2.
2. Reader 2 Begins	Reader 2 reads the story to Reader 1.
3. Reread	For optimal fluency, students should reread three to four times.
4. Provide Feedback	Listen to students read and provide corrective feedback regarding their fluency and their decoding.

For additional practice, use "Carla's Big Project" on Worktext p. 19.

Fluency Lesson 4
Rate 2

Objectives:

- Read at a speed that resembles natural speech.

MATERIALS

Worktext pp. 20–25
Routine Cards 2, 8
Leveled Reader Database

Set the scene Review rate with students. Connect it to a familiar task, such as singing. When we sing together, we don't sing too fast or too slow. The same thing happens when we read. We don't rush through a story or read it too slowly. Explain to students that they should read as if they were talking to a friend. Tell students that by practicing to read this way, they can become better readers.

Model and teach Introduce the story "Music Class" on Worktext p. 20. We will read the story at the same speed we use when we talk to a friend. When we are finished reading, I will ask you a question about the story.

Ask students if they know what a *recorder* is. Note that this word has more than one meaning. One meaning is "a machine that records sounds." In this story, a recorder is a musical instrument. Show students a real recorder or a photograph of one.

- Explain to students that you will read the first paragraph aloud. I will read in a way that sounds like I am talking to you.
- Remind students that reading silently before they read aloud will help them become familiar with the words. Pause a few moments to read to yourself.

Have students follow along as you model reading the first paragraph at a speed that students will recognize as natural speech. Then read it again too fast or too slow. Discuss with students which reading was easier to understand and why.

Check comprehension What instrument does Mr. Riley give to each student? (a recorder)

Fluency Goal: 80–105 words correct per minute

Remind students that...

- they should read the story at the same speed they would speak to a friend.
- they should pause when they see a period and make their voice go up when they see a question mark.
- reading each paragraph to themselves will help familiarize them with the words.

Guide Practice

Discuss the story "Music Class" on Worktext p. 20. Write the words *instruments, recorder, different,* and *sounds.* Point to each word as you read it aloud. Have students read the words aloud with you and without you.

Give students time to read the second paragraph silently. Then read aloud with them, modeling a natural rate.

If... students cannot read a word,
then... have them blend decodable words **(Routine Card 2)** or say and spell high-frequency words **(Routine Card 8)**.

On Their Own Prepare students for a choral reading of "Music Class." You are going to read the story aloud as a group. Try to read at a natural rate.

Routine	Choral Reading
1. Read Together	Have students read aloud with you.
2. Reread	Then have students read aloud without you. For optimal fluency, students should reread three to four times.
3. Provide Feedback	Listen to students read and provide corrective feedback.

If students read the passage fluently, provide additional practice by assigning "Basketball Practice" on Worktext p. 21.

Fluency Goal: 100–125 words correct per minute
Remind students that…

- they should read at the same speed that they speak.
- reading silently before reading aloud will help them become familiar with the words.
- quotation marks show that characters are speaking.

Guide Practice
Introduce the story "Be Polite, Please!" on Worktext p. 22. Review quotation marks. Quotation marks tell us exactly what a character says. Point out quotation marks throughout the story.

Read the first two paragraphs for students, making sure to change your voice when you come to a direct quotation. Then give students time to read the same paragraphs silently and then aloud.

If… students are reading too slowly or they're halting, **then…** model a sentence at a natural pace and ask them to echo you. Repeat three or four more times.

On Their Own Pair students to do an oral reading of "Be Polite, Please!"

Routine	Paired Reading
1. Reader 1 Begins	Reader 1 reads the story to Reader 2.
2. Reader 2 Begins	Reader 2 reads the story to Reader 1.
3. Reread	For optimal fluency, students should reread three to four times.
4. Provide Feedback	Listen to students read and provide corrective feedback.

For additional practice, have students read "George Washington" on Worktext p. 23 with a partner.

Mini-Lesson 3

Fluency Goal: 120–145 words correct per minute
Remind students that…

- they should read at the same speed that they would speak.
- reading silently before reading aloud will help them become familiar with the words.
- they should read neither too fast nor too slow.

Guide Practice
Tell students "Cynthia Rylant: A Writer's Story" on Worktext p. 24 is a nonfiction passage about a real writer of children's books. Give students time to read the first paragraph silently, and then read aloud with them. Model reading the passage at an appropriate rate. Change your voice when reading a quotation.

If… students are reading too quickly, **then…** ask them to read at the rate they use when talking. Model a sentence slowly and have students repeat. Gradually increase speed until all students are reading together and at a normal pace.

On Their Own Pair students to do an oral reading of "Cynthia Rylant: A Writer's Story."

Routine	Paired Reading
1. Reader 1 Begins	Reader 1 reads the story to Reader 2.
2. Reader 2 Begins	Reader 2 reads the story to Reader 1.
3. Reread	For optimal fluency, students should reread three to four times.
4. Provide Feedback	Listen to students read and provide corrective feedback regarding their fluency and their decoding.

For additional practice, use "Ramon's Book" on Worktext p. 25.

Fluency Lesson 5

Accuracy and Rate 1

Objectives:

- Read fluently without errors, at a rate that you recognize as natural speech.

MATERIALS

Worktext pp. 26–31
Routine Cards 2, 8
Leveled Reader Database

Set the scene Review the concepts of accuracy and rate. Explain to students that this lesson will focus on reading without mistakes at a natural pace. Students will learn to read carefully, pacing themselves so that they do not rush and mispronounce words. Tell students that using a natural reading rate sounds like you are talking.

Model and teach Introduce the story "The Big Tree" on p. 26. Tell students that they will be practicing two skills at once today. They should read every word accurately and not read too fast or too slow. Then review exclamation marks. There are exclamation marks in some of the sentences. Remember to show surprise or excitement with your voice when you see an exclamation mark.

- Tell students that you will read the first two sentences aloud. I want to read without making any mistakes. I want to make sure that I am not reading too fast or too slow. I will show excitement or surprise with my voice when I see an exclamation mark.
- Remind students that they need to be familiar with the words to read accurately. Reading silently before reading aloud will help them learn how to pronounce new words. Model by pausing to read to yourself.

Have students follow along as you model reading the first two sentences.

Check comprehension Who tells Joel to be careful? (his mom)

Fluency Goal: 20–45 words correct per minute

Remind students that...

- they should read every word in the passage and read words correctly.
- reading too fast or too slow will make their reading difficult to understand.
- exclamation marks mean that they should show surprise or excitement in their voices.

Guide Practice

Discuss the story "The Big Tree" on p. 26. Give students time to read the next three sentences silently. Then have students read the sentences aloud with you. Continue in this way for the remaining sentences. Remind students to show excitement or surprise when they read a sentence ending in an exclamation mark.

If... students cannot read a word,
then... have them blend decodable words **(Routine Card 2)** or say and spell high-frequency words **(Routine Card 8)**.

On Their Own Prepare the group for a choral reading of "The Big Tree." You are going to read the story aloud as a group. Remember to read every word and try to read all the words correctly. Speak at the same speed you would talk to a friend.

Routine	**Choral Reading**
1. Read Together	Have students read aloud with you.
2. Reread	Then have students read aloud without you. For optimal fluency, students should reread three to four times.
3. Provide Feedback	Listen to students and provide corrective feedback.

For additional practice, use "Ouch!" on p. 27.

Mini-Lesson 2

Fluency Goal: 40–65 words correct per minute

Remind students that...

- they should read every word accurately.
- a natural reading rate sounds like they are talking to a friend.
- reading the story silently first will help them become familiar with the words.

Guide Practice

Introduce the story "A Day at the Amusement Park" on p. 28. Be sure students know what a roller coaster is. Ask if students have ever been on one. Next, give students time to read the first paragraph silently. Then read the paragraph aloud with students, paying special attention to accuracy and rate.

If... students cannot hear the difference in rate as they read,

then... model reading a few sentences three different ways. First, read too slowly. Next, read too quickly. Finally, read at the rate of natural speech. Ask students to tell you which sounds the most like the way people talk.

On Their Own Pair students to do an oral reading of "A Day at the Amusement Park."

Routine	Paired Reading
1. Reader 1 Begins	Reader 1 reads the story to Reader 2.
2. Reader 2 Begins	Reader 2 reads the story to Reader 1.
3. Reread	For optimal fluency, students should reread three to four times.
4. Provide Feedback	Listen to students read and provide corrective feedback.

For additional practice, use "Mount Rushmore" on p. 29.

Mini-Lesson 3

Fluency Goal: 60–85 words correct per minute

Remind students that...

- they should read every word accurately and not skip over or substitute words.
- they should read at a rate that sounds like they are talking to a friend.
- skipping or substituting words may change the meaning of a sentence.

Guide Practice

Introduce the story "The Mystery of the Disappearing Friends" on p. 30. Remind students that skipping or substituting words can change the meaning of a sentence. Have students follow along as you model reading the first paragraph accurately and at a natural pace. Then have students read the next paragraph aloud with you.

If... students have trouble reading difficult words,

then... point to the words, read them aloud, and then model reading the sentences that contain these words. Have students echo your modeling.

On Their Own Pair students to do an oral reading of "The Mystery of the Disappearing Friends."

Routine	Paired Reading
1. Reader 1 Begins	Reader 1 reads the story to Reader 2.
2. Reader 2 Begins	Reader 2 reads the story to Reader 1.
3. Reread	For optimal fluency, students should reread three to four times.
4. Provide Feedback	Listen to students read and provide corrective feedback regarding their fluency and their decoding.

For additional practice, use "Double Trouble!" on p. 31.

Fluency Lesson 6

Accuracy and Rate 2

Objectives:

- Read fluently without errors, at the same rate at which you would speak.

MATERIALS

Worktext pp. 32–37
Routine Cards 2, 8
Leveled Reader Database

Set the scene Review the concepts of accuracy and rate. Explain that when you listen to someone read aloud, you don't want the reader to rush or read too slowly. You want to be able to hear each word read just the way it was written. Today students will practice two skills—reading every word correctly and reading at a natural speed. Explain that they will practice until they can read without mistakes. The more you practice, the more you will find it becomes easier to read well aloud.

Model and teach Introduce the story "The Last Day of School" on p. 32. Ask students what they did on their last day of school last year. When you have finished reading the story, I will ask you a question about it.

Remind students to pay attention to punctuation when they read at a natural pace. They should pause briefly when they see commas. They should pause slightly longer for periods.

- Tell students that you will read the first paragraph aloud without making any mistakes. You will read in a way that sounds as if you are talking to them. You will take care to not read too fast or too slow.
- Explain that you will read the paragraph silently to yourself before you read it aloud. This helps you become familiar with the words. Model by pausing to read to yourself.

Have students follow along as you model reading the first paragraph with no mistakes and at a pace that students will recognize as natural speech.

Check comprehension What kind of questions does Mr. Burns ask? (He asks questions about what the students learned.)

Fluency Goal: 80–105 words correct per minute

Remind students that...

- they should read every word in the passage and read words correctly.
- reading as if they are talking makes the text easier to understand.
- they should read silently to become familiar with the words.

Guide Practice

Continue modeling accuracy and rate in "The Last Day of School" on p. 32. Give students time to read the second paragraph silently before they read it aloud. Remind students not to read too quickly or too slowly.

If... students cannot read a word,
then... have them blend decodable words **(Routine Card 2)** or say and spell high-frequency words **(Routine Card 8).**

On Their Own Prepare the group for a choral reading of "The Last Day of School." You are going to read the story aloud as a group. Read every word correctly. Speak at the same speed you would talk to someone.

Routine	**Choral Reading**
1. Read Together	Have students read aloud with you.
2. Reread	Then have students read aloud without you. For optimal fluency, students should reread three to four times.
3. Provide Feedback	Listen to students read and provide corrective feedback.

For additional practice, use "The Princess and the Frog" on p. 33.

Mini-Lesson 2

Fluency Goal: 100–125 words correct per minute

Remind students that...

- they should read every word accurately without skipping or substituting words.
- reading too fast or too slow makes reading harder to understand.

Guide Practice

Introduce "Into the Darkness" on p. 34. Point to the words *bedtime, goodnight,* and *downstairs* as you read them aloud. Then have students follow along as you model fluent reading of the sentences containing these words. Read the first paragraph aloud with students. Explain that you are reading at a pace that is neither too fast nor too slow.

If... students substitute a word or make a mistake,

then... point to the misidentified word, sound it out, and then read it correctly. Then model the entire sentence and have them repeat it until they are fluent.

On Their Own Pair students to do an oral reading of "Into the Darkness."

Routine	Paired Reading
1. Reader 1 Begins	Reader 1 reads the story to Reader 2.
2. Reader 2 Begins	Reader 2 reads the story to Reader 1.
3. Reread	For optimal fluency, students should reread three to four times.
4. Provide Feedback	Listen to students read and provide corrective feedback.

For additional practice, use "Nathan the Great" on p. 35.

Mini-Lesson 3

Fluency Goal: 120–145 words correct per minute

Remind students that...

- they should read every word accurately and at a good pace.
- they should take a moment to read the paragraphs to themselves.
- they should show excitement or surprise when they see an exclamation mark.

Guide Practice

Introduce "Birthday Cake" on p. 36. Then have students follow along as you model reading the first paragraph. First, model reading too slowly with mistakes. Then read fluently. Ask students which reading was easier to understand. Give students time to read the second paragraph silently, and then read it aloud with them.

If... students are reading too fast or too slow,

then... ask them to listen to you as you read at a normal pace. Then have students echo your reading, first reading with you and then reading without you.

On Their Own Pair students to do an oral reading of "Birthday Cake."

Routine	Paired Reading
1. Reader 1 Begins	Reader 1 reads the story to Reader 2.
2. Reader 2 Begins	Reader 2 reads the story to Reader 1.
3. Reread	For optimal fluency, students should reread three to four times.
4. Provide Feedback	Listen to students read and provide corrective feedback regarding their fluency and their decoding.

For additional practice, use "The Reading Contest" on p. 37.

Fluency Lesson 7

Accuracy and Rate 3

Objectives:

- Read fluently without errors, at a speed you recognize as natural speech.

MATERIALS

Worktext pp. 38–43
Routine Cards 2, 8
Leveled Reader Database

Set the scene Review accuracy and rate. Today we will practice reading carefully and reading neither too fast nor too slow. The more you practice, the better your reading will become.

Model and teach Introduce the story "The Broken Plates" on p. 38. Remind students that accidents happen. Being careful will reduce the number of accidents we have. When we have finished reading, I will ask you a question about the story.

Ask students if any words stand out in the text. They may notice that one word in the story is in all capital letters. Tell students that when an author wants to emphasize a word, the author might put the word in all capital letters. We should read these words louder to make them stand out.

- Before you read the first paragraph aloud, tell students that you want to read without making any mistakes. You will read at a normal pace, as if you are speaking to someone. If a word is in all capital letters, you will read the word louder to make it stand out.
- Tell students that you will first read the paragraph silently to become familiar with the words. Pause to read to yourself.

Have students follow along as you model reading the first paragraph with no mistakes. Focus on not reading too fast or too slow. Read words in all capital letters slightly louder for emphasis.

Check comprehension Why does Salim drop the plates? (His dog runs in front of him.)

Fluency Goal: 20–45 words correct per minute

Remind students that…

- they should read every word in the story and read words correctly.
- not reading too fast or too slow will make their reading easier to understand.
- words in all capital letters are important and should be read louder.

Guide Practice

Discuss the story "The Broken Plates" on p. 38. Remind students to focus on reading each word correctly at a speed that sounds like natural speech. Read words in all capital letters louder. Give students time to read the paragraph silently, and then have them read it aloud.

If… students cannot read a word,
then… have them blend decodable words **(Routine Card 2)** or say and spell high-frequency words **(Routine Card 8)**.

On Their Own Prepare the group for a choral reading of "The Broken Plates." You are going to read the story aloud as a group. Read carefully. Don't leave out or change any words. Read at a speed that sounds like talking.

Routine	Choral Reading
1. Read Together	Have students read aloud with you.
2. Reread	Then have students read aloud without you. For optimal fluency, students should reread three to four times.
3. Provide Feedback	Listen to students and provide corrective feedback.

If students read the passage fluently, provide additional practice by assigning "Car Trip" on p. 39.

Mini-Lesson 2

Fluency Goal: 40–65 words correct per minute

Remind students that...

- they should read every word accurately without skipping or substituting any words.
- reading too fast or too slow will make their reading harder to understand.
- reading sentences silently first will help them become familiar with the words.

Guide Practice

Introduce the story "Bowling" on p. 40. Point out and define bowling terms for students who may not be familiar with the game. Explain terms such as *pins, spare,* and *strike.* Then have students follow along as you model reading the first paragraph, paying particular attention to modeling a normal rate. Give students time to read the second paragraph silently. Then have students read aloud with you.

If... students are reading too quickly or too slowly,
then... ask them to read at the rate they use when talking. Model the first sentence slowly and have students repeat. Gradually increase speed until all students are reading at a normal pace.

On Their Own Pair students to do an oral reading of "Bowling."

Routine	Paired Reading
1. Reader 1 Begins	Reader 1 reads the story to Reader 2.
2. Reader 2 Begins	Reader 2 reads the story to Reader 1.
3. Reread	For optimal fluency, students should reread three to four times.
4. Provide Feedback	Listen to students read and provide corrective feedback. Point out any words students skip over or read incorrectly.

For additional practice, use "Aunt Carrie" on p. 41.

Mini-Lesson 3

Fluency Goal: 60–85 words correct per minute

Remind students that...

- they should read every word in the story.
- skipping or substituting words can change the meaning of a sentence.
- a reading rate that resembles natural speech is easiest to understand.

Guide Practice

Introduce the story "The Catch" on p. 42. Make sure that students are familiar with baseball terms, such as *left field* and *glove.* If they are not sure where left field is, draw a diagram of a baseball diamond and point out left field. Give students time to read the paragraph silently. Then have students read the first paragraph aloud with you. Model reading accurately at a normal rate of speed.

If... students skip over words,
then... have them track the print as they practice. Then have them read the story without tracking.

On Their Own Pair students to do an oral reading of "The Catch."

Routine	Paired Reading
1. Reader 1 Begins	Reader 1 reads the story to Reader 2.
2. Reader 2 Begins	Reader 2 reads the story to Reader 1.
3. Reread	For optimal fluency, students should reread three to four times.
4. Provide Feedback	Listen to students read and provide corrective feedback regarding their fluency and their decoding.

For additional practice, use "Paul the Painter" on p. 43.

Fluency Lesson 8

Accuracy and Rate 4

Objectives:

- Read the words in a text correctly.
- Read at a natural rate.

MATERIALS

Worktext pp. 44–49
Leveled Reader Database

Set the scene Review the concepts of accuracy and rate. Today we will practice reading all the words in a passage correctly while reading at the natural speed we use when talking. That means we won't read too fast or too slow. Practicing these skills will make us better readers.

Model and teach Introduce the story "Take a Hike!" on p. 44. Remind students that reading accurately means reading every word correctly. Explain to students that reading the story silently before reading it aloud will help students become familiar with the words. When they know the words, they can read at a speed listeners will recognize as natural speech.

- Tell students that you will read the paragraph to yourself before you read it aloud with them. Pause to read to yourself.
- Tell students that you want to read without making any mistakes. You will read in a way that sounds like you are talking to them, not too fast or too slow. Read the first paragraph aloud.

Have students follow along as you model reading the first paragraph with no mistakes at a natural rate.

Check comprehension In two to three sentences, summarize what happens in this story. (Sasha and her mother take a hike up a hill. They will have lunch at a picnic area at the top of the hill. They can see the lake from the top.)

Mini-Lesson 1

Fluency Goal: 80–105 words correct per minute

Remind students that...

- they should read every word in the passage and read words correctly.
- they should read at the same speed that they would talk to a friend.

Guide Practice

Discuss "Take a Hike!" on p. 44. Model reading the second paragraph accurately and at a natural pace. Point out that skipping or substituting words will change the meaning of sentences. Then give students time to read the paragraph silently. Have students read the second paragraph aloud with you.

If... many students substitute or misread a particular word,
then... pronounce the word and have students repeat it several times before reading it in context.

On Their Own Prepare the group for a choral reading of "Take a Hike!" You are going to read the story aloud as a group. Read carefully and don't leave out or change any words. Read at a natural speed.

Routine	Choral Reading
1. Read Together	Have students read aloud with you.
2. Reread	Then have students read aloud without you. For optimal fluency, students should reread three to four times.
3. Provide Feedback	Listen to students and provide corrective feedback.

If students read the passage fluently, provide additional practice by assigning "Weather" on p. 45.

Mini-Lesson 2

Fluency Goal: 100–125 words correct per minute
Remind students that...

- reading every word accurately will make their reading easier to understand.
- they should read at the same speed that they normally talk.
- skipping or substituting words will change the meaning of sentences.

Guide Practice
Introduce the story "Sunflowers" on p. 46. Have students follow along as you model reading the first paragraph without mistakes and at a rate that resembles natural speech. Give students time to read the paragraph silently. Then have students read the next paragraph aloud with you.

If... students skip a word,
then... have them track selected text until they read accurately. If they substitute a word, point to the word, sound it out, and read it correctly. Then model the sentence and have students repeat it.

On Their Own Pair students to do an oral reading of "Sunflowers."

Routine	**Paired Reading**
1. Reader 1 Begins	Reader 1 reads the passage to Reader 2.
2. Reader 2 Begins	Reader 2 reads the passage to Reader 1.
3. Reread	For optimal fluency, students should reread three to four times.
4. Provide Feedback	Listen to students read and provide corrective feedback. Point out any words students skip over or read incorrectly.

For additional practice, have students read "The Greatest Soccer Player You Will Ever Meet" on p. 47.

Mini-Lesson 3

Fluency Goal: 120–145 words correct per minute
Remind students that...

- they should read every word in the story accurately.
- they should read at a natural rate, neither too fast nor too slow.

Guide Practice
Introduce "Summer's New Bicycle" on p. 48. Model reading the first paragraph aloud. Remind students that skipping or substituting words can change the meaning of the passage. Have students read the paragraph silently, and then have them read aloud with you.

If... students are reading very slowly,
then... encourage them to read the passage silently several times so that the words become familiar. After that, have them read the passage aloud at a natural speaking rate.

On Their Own Have students form groups of three to do a reading performance of "Summer's New Bicycle." Assign one student to be the narrator and a different student to read each speaking part (Summer and her mother). Then have each group read the story aloud to the class.

Routine	**Reading Performance**
1. Read Silently	Students read their parts silently.
2. Read Together	Each reader performs his or her assigned part.
3. Reread	Students should track the print as they listen. For optimal fluency, students should reread three to four times.
4. Provide Feedback	Listen to students read and provide corrective feedback regarding their fluency and decoding.

For additional practice, use "Zoo Trip" on p. 49.

Fluency Lesson 9
Appropriate Phrasing/Punctuation Cues 1

Objectives:

- Attend to punctuation while reading, pausing in appropriate places.
- Group words into meaningful phrases when reading.

MATERIALS

Worktext pp. 50–55
Leveled Reader Database

Set the scene Introduce punctuation cues and appropriate phrasing. Explain that punctuation cues, such as commas and periods, tell when to pause while reading. Appropriate phrasing means grouping words together so they make sense while reading.

Model and teach Introduce the story "Blue's Bubble Bath" on p. 50. Explain that phrases are groups of words that relate to each other, such as "my little sister" and "by tomorrow morning." When you see phrases, read them together, not word by word. Then tell students that punctuation marks are clues that tell where to pause in a sentence. Commas help us figure out how to divide the sentences into phrases as we read. You should pause briefly when you come to a comma. Pause slightly longer at the end of sentences. Tell students that sentences end in end marks: periods, question marks, or exclamation marks.

- Explain to students that you will read the sentences silently first to help you become familiar with the words. Model by pausing to read to yourself.
- Then tell students that you will read the first three sentences aloud, grouping words together so they make sense and pausing after each comma.

Have students follow along as you model reading the first three sentences.

Check comprehension What happens when Ruby pours bubbles in the water? (Blue chases the bubbles and jumps in the water.)

Fluency Goal: 20–45 words correct per minute
Remind students that…

- commas indicate that they should pause briefly.
- they should group words into phrases that make sense.
- they should read every word in the passage accurately and read at a natural pace.

Guide Practice
Discuss the story "Blue's Bubble Bath" on p. 50. Give students time to read the next three sentences silently. Then read the sentences aloud, reading word by word and with awkward pausing. Discuss the problems with the reading. Then read the story aloud again, modeling appropriate phrasing. Finally, have students read aloud with you.

If… students have trouble pausing for punctuation, **then…** first have them circle the punctuation on their copies before they read. Remind them to pause slightly for commas and longer for end marks.

On Their Own Prepare the group for a choral reading of "Blue's Bubble Bath." You are going to read the story aloud as a group. As you read, watch for commas and group the words together in phrases that make sense.

Routine	Choral Reading
1. Read Together	Have students read aloud with you.
2. Reread	Then have students read aloud without you. For optimal fluency, students should reread three to four times.
3. Provide Feedback	Listen to students read and provide corrective feedback.

If students read the passage fluently, provide additional practice by assigning "Spelling Bee" on p. 51.

Mini-Lesson 2

Fluency Goal: 40–65 words correct per minute

Remind students that...

- commas show where students should pause briefly.
- they should group words into meaningful phrases as they read.
- they should read every word accurately and at a natural rate.

Guide Practice

Introduce "Ice Cream" on p. 52. Have students follow along as you model reading the first two sentences, pausing briefly for commas and paying particular attention to grouping words based on meaning. Before having students read the next two sentences aloud, give them time to read the sentences silently.

If... students are pausing inappropriately within phrases,
then... explain why particular groups of words, such as compound nouns or prepositional phrases, should be read together. Model appropriate phrasing, and have students echo three or four times.

On Their Own Pair students to do an oral reading of "Ice Cream."

Routine	**Paired Reading**
1. Reader 1 Begins	Reader 1 reads the story to Reader 2.
2. Reader 2 Begins	Reader 2 reads the story to Reader 1.
3. Reread	For optimal fluency, students should reread three to four times.
4. Provide Feedback	Listen to students read and provide corrective feedback. Point out if students are not grouping words or pausing appropriately.

Provide additional practice by having students read "School Shopping" on p. 53 with a partner.

Mini-Lesson 3

Fluency Goal: 60–85 words correct per minute

Remind students that...

- commas signal a short pause in a sentence.
- they should group words into meaningful phrases as they read.
- to become familiar with the words in a passage, they can read the passage silently before reading it aloud.

Guide Practice

Introduce "The Yard Sale" on p. 54. Have students follow along as you model reading the first paragraph. Have students read the paragraph silently. Then have them read the paragraph aloud with you.

If... students have difficulty understanding how phrasing affects meaning,
then... read several sentences without pausing or grouping words together. Discuss how the meaning is not clear. Next, read the sentences correctly and have students repeat after you.

On Their Own Pair students to do an oral reading of "The Yard Sale."

Routine	**Paired Reading**
1. Reader 1 Begins	Reader 1 reads the story to Reader 2.
2. Reader 2 Begins	Reader 2 reads the story to Reader 1.
3. Reread	For optimal fluency, students should reread three to four times.
4. Provide Feedback	Listen to students read and provide corrective feedback regarding their phrasing.

For additional practice, use "Learning to Swim" on p. 55.

Fluency Lesson 10

Appropriate Phrasing/Punctuation Cues 2

Objectives:

- Attend to punctuation cues while reading, pausing in appropriate places.
- Group words meaningfully when reading.

MATERIALS

Worktext pp. 56–61
Leveled Reader Database

Set the scene Review phrasing. Reading with appropriate phrasing means reading chunks or groups of words instead of just reading word by word. We will practice grouping words correctly and pausing when we come to commas.

Model and teach Introduce the story "One Day in the Big City" on p. 56. Point out New York City on a map and explain that it is one of the largest cities in the world. Then discuss phrases with students. Some sentences have commas. Commas help us divide sentences into phrases. Phrases are groups of related words. Sometimes phrases are not separated by commas. When sentences do not have commas, think about the meaning of the words as you read each sentence silently. Write the following sentence: *On Saturday mornings, my dad and I run in the park.* Which words are related? (on Saturday mornings, my dad and I run, in the park)

- Before reading aloud, explain that you will read the paragraph silently to help you become familiar with the words and how you should read the phrases.
- Then tell students that you will read the first paragraph aloud. I want to group the words as I read instead of reading word by word. I will pause briefly when I read a comma.

Have students follow along as you model reading the first paragraph.

Check comprehension How does Megan feel about going on the trip? (Megan is excited and scared.)

Fluency Goal: 80–105 words correct per minute

Remind students that...

- commas tell the reader to pause briefly.
- they should group words into phrases that make sense as they read.
- they should read every word in the passage correctly and at a natural rate.

Guide Practice

Introduce the story "One Day in the Big City" on p. 56. Then give students time to read the next three sentences silently before having them read them aloud with you. As you read aloud with students, model appropriate phrasing.

If... students tend to read word by word,
then... model reading a paragraph by grouping words meaningfully. Point out how you grouped words and why.

On Their Own Prepare the group for a choral reading of "One Day in the Big City." You are going to read the story aloud as a group. Pause briefly when you see a comma and group words as you read.

Routine	Choral Reading
1. Read Together	Have students read aloud with you.
2. Reread	Then have students read aloud without you. For optimal fluency, students should reread three to four times.
3. Provide Feedback	Listen to students read and provide corrective feedback. Point out any words students skip over or read incorrectly.

For additional practice, use "The Best Brother Ever" on p. 57.

Mini-Lesson 2

Fluency Goal: 100–125 words correct per minute

Remind students that...

- they should pause briefly when they see a comma.
- they can look for related words to help them group words together.
- they should read accurately and at a natural rate.

Guide Practice

Introduce the story "Naveed's Favorite Uncle" on p. 58. Have students follow along as you model reading the first paragraph, pausing briefly for commas and paying particular attention to grouping words. Give students time to read the next three sentences silently. Then read the sentences aloud with them.

If... students cannot read fluently without you,
then... have them finish reading the story with you before reading in pairs.

On Their Own Pair students to do an oral reading of "Naveed's Favorite Uncle."

Routine	Paired Reading
1. Reader 1 Begins	Reader 1 reads the story to Reader 2.
2. Reader 2 Begins	Reader 2 reads the story to Reader 1.
3. Reread	For optimal fluency, students should reread three to four times.
4. Provide Feedback	Listen to students read and provide corrective feedback. Point out any words students skip over or read incorrectly. Also point out if they read word by word or miss punctuation cues.

Provide additional practice by having students read "Which Instrument Will You Learn to Play?" on p. 59 with a partner.

Mini-Lesson 3

Fluency Goal: 120–145 words correct per minute

Remind students that...

- commas signal a short pause in a sentence.
- grouping words into phrases that make sense will help listeners better understand and enjoy the reading.
- they should read accurately and at a natural rate.

Guide Practice

Introduce "The Nature Walk" on p. 60. Write the following words on the board: *nature, chipmunk, mushrooms,* and *beautiful.* Check that students know the meaning and pronunciation of each. Then have students follow along as you model reading the first paragraph, emphasizing pausing for punctuation and grouping words meaningfully. Finally, have students read the paragraph silently before reading it aloud together.

If... students group words awkwardly or pause inappropriately when no punctuation cues are present,
then... read a sentence, emphasizing awkward phrasing. Guide students to see that it is difficult to understand what was read. Then read the sentence again with correct phrasing and have students repeat until they are fluent.

On Their Own Pair students to do an oral reading of "The Nature Walk."

Routine	Paired Reading
1. Reader 1 Begins	Reader 1 reads the story to Reader 2.
2. Reader 2 Begins	Reader 2 reads the story to Reader 1.
3. Reread	For optimal fluency, students should reread three to four times.
4. Provide Feedback	Listen to students read and provide corrective feedback.

For additional practice, use "Making Maple Candy" on p. 61.

Fluency Lesson 11

Appropriate Phrasing/Punctuation Cues 3

Objectives:

- Use punctuation cues to help group words while reading.
- Group words into meaningful phrases when reading.

MATERIALS

Worktext pp. 62–67
Routine Cards 2, 8
Leveled Reader Database

Set the scene Review punctuation and phrasing with students. Explain that they can use clues, such as commas, to figure out where to pause. With oral practice, students will find that reading with correct phrasing becomes easier.

Model and teach Introduce the reading passage "Seeds" on p. 62. Check that students are familiar with the story of Johnny Appleseed. Tell students that some sentences contain punctuation clues, such as commas, that show how to group words. In addition, they must figure out how to group words into phrases based on meaning, even if there is no punctuation. For example, words like *and* and *or* can show when words should be grouped together. *(Raul and Mary go up the stairs.)* Words such as *up, inside,* and *on* are often part of phrases that should be read as a group. *(Raul and Mary go up the stairs.)*

- **Prepare to read the first two sentences aloud.** As I read, I will group words together in phrases that make sense and pause briefly for commas.
- **Tell students that you will first read the sentences silently to help you become familiar with the words. Pause to read to yourself.**

Have students follow along as you model reading the first two sentences.

Check comprehension Where does Johnny carry his seeds? **(Johnny carries seeds in his pack.)**

Fluency Goal: 20–45 words correct per minute
Remind students that...

- they should pause briefly for commas.
- they can first read sentences silently to help them become familiar with the words.
- they should read every word in the passage correctly and read at a natural pace.

Guide Practice
Discuss "Seeds" on p. 62. Before having students read the next two sentences aloud with you, have them read the sentences silently. Then read the sentences with students.

If... students cannot read a particular word,
then... have them blend decodable words **(Routine Card 2)** or say and spell high-frequency words **(Routine Card 8).**

On Their Own Prepare the group for a choral reading of "Seeds." You are going to read the story aloud as a group. Read carefully and don't leave out or change any words. As you read, pause briefly when you see a comma and group words instead of reading word by word.

Routine	**Choral Reading**
1. Read Together	Have students read aloud with you.
2. Reread	Then have students read aloud without you. For optimal fluency, students should reread three to four times.
3. Provide Feedback	Listen to students read and provide corrective feedback.

If students read the passage fluently, provide additional practice by assigning "Mules" on p. 63.

Mini-Lesson 2

Fluency Goal: 40–65 words correct per minute
Remind students that...

- they should pause briefly at commas.
- they should group words into meaningful phrases.
- they should read every word accurately at a natural pace.

Guide Practice
Introduce "Cousins" on p. 64. Have students follow along as you model reading the first three sentences, pausing briefly for commas and paying particular attention to grouping words according to meaning. Give students time to read the next three sentences silently. Then have students read the sentences aloud with you.

If... students have difficulty with phrasing where commas are present,
then... make sure students can identify commas in selected text. Point out the commas if necessary. Model reading the text, pausing at commas, and have students echo read three or four times.

On Their Own Pair students to do an oral reading of "Cousins."

Routine	**Paired Reading**
1. Reader 1 Begins	Reader 1 reads the passage to Reader 2.
2. Reader 2 Begins	Reader 2 reads the passage to Reader 1.
3. Reread	For optimal fluency, students should reread three to four times.
4. Provide Feedback	Listen to students read and provide corrective feedback. Point out if students are not grouping words correctly.

For additional practice, assign "Rummage Sale" on p. 65.

Mini-Lesson 3

Fluency Goal: 60–85 words correct per minute
Remind students that...

- they should pause slightly for commas in a sentence.
- they can group words into meaningful phrases to make their reading easier to understand.
- they should read every word accurately and at a natural pace.

Guide Practice
Introduce "The Deer" on p. 66. Have students follow along as you model reading the first paragraph, pausing within phrases and ignoring punctuation cues. Ask students if the paragraph was difficult to understand and why. Then give students time to read the paragraph silently. Read the paragraph aloud with students, modeling appropriate phrasing.

If... students have difficulty with phrasing,
then... read selected text, reading the words one by one. Then read with appropriate phrasing and have students echo read three or four times.

On Their Own Pair students to do an oral reading of "The Deer."

Routine	**Paired Reading**
1. Reader 1 Begins	Reader 1 reads the story to Reader 2.
2. Reader 2 Begins	Reader 2 reads the story to Reader 1.
3. Reread	For optimal fluency, students should reread three to four times.
4. Provide Feedback	Listen to students read and provide corrective feedback regarding their fluency and their decoding.

For additional practice, assign "Soccer Rules!" on p. 67.

Fluency Lesson 12

Appropriate Phrasing/Punctuation Cues 4

Objectives:

- Use punctuation cues to help group words while reading.
- Group words into meaningful phrases when reading.

MATERIALS

Worktext pp. 68–73
Routine Cards 2, 8
Leveled Reader Database

Set the scene Review punctuation cues and phrasing with students. Today we will practice correct phrasing, or how to group words together while reading a sentence. As we read, think about reading groups of words instead of just reading word by word. We will also focus on how commas and quotation marks affect how we read groups of words. Reading with correct phrasing makes it easier to understand a passage.

Model and teach Introduce the reading passage "The New Student" on p. 68. Explain that the story tells about a boy who moves from Somalia. Point out Somalia on a map. Remind students to group words together as they read. Point out that some words are grouped in quotation marks, which show dialogue.

- Prepare to read the first paragraph aloud. Explain that you will group words together in phrases that make sense and pause for commas.
- Before I read aloud, I will read the sentences to myself. This helps me become familiar with the words. Pause to read to yourself.

Have students follow along as you model reading the first paragraph.

Check comprehension In two to three sentences, summarize what happens in this story. (Miss Lee introduces Abdi to the class. He is from Somalia. The class asks Abdi questions about Somalia.)

Fluency Goal: 80–105 words correct per minute

Remind students that…

- they can use punctuation cues to help them group words.
- they should group words into phrases that make sense.
- they should read every word in the passage correctly and read at a natural pace.

Guide Practice

Continue modeling phrasing and punctuation cues with "The New Student" on p. 68. Tell students to read the second paragraph silently and then read it aloud with them. Address any difficulties with phrasing and have students echo read as you model correct phrasing.

If… students cannot read a word,
then… have them blend decodable words **(Routine Card 2)** or say and spell high-frequency words **(Routine Card 8)**.

On Their Own Prepare the group for a choral reading of "The New Student." You are going to read the story aloud as a group. As you read, pause for commas and group together words into phrases that make sense.

Routine	**Choral Reading**
1. Read Together **2. Reread**	Have students read aloud with you. Then have students read aloud without you. For optimal fluency, students should reread three to four times.
3. Provide Feedback	Listen to students read and provide corrective feedback.

For additional practice, use "Annie's New Uniform" on p. 69.

Mini-Lesson 2

Fluency Goal: 100–125 words correct per minute

Remind students that...

- they should group words into phrases that make sense as they read.
- they should use punctuation clues, such as quotation marks, to help group words as they read.
- they should read every word accurately at a natural rate.

Guide Practice

Introduce the story "Jasmine Changes Her Mind" on p. 70. Then discuss quotation marks. Quotation marks show when someone is speaking. Read the words inside quotation marks together. For long text inside quotation marks, use punctuation cues and group words into meaningful phrases. Model reading the first paragraph. Have students read the second paragraph silently. Then read it aloud with them.

If... students have difficulty understanding how phrasing affects meaning,
then... read a sentence with dialogue without pausing or grouping words together. Discuss how the meaning is not clear. Then read the sentence correctly and have students repeat after you.

On Their Own Pair students to do an oral reading of "Jasmine Changes Her Mind."

Routine	Paired Reading
1. Reader 1 Begins	Reader 1 reads the story to Reader 2.
2. Reader 2 Begins	Reader 2 reads the story to Reader 1.
3. Reread	For optimal fluency, students should reread three to four times.
4. Provide Feedback	Listen to students read and provide corrective feedback.

For additional practice, use "The Silent Storyteller" on p. 71.

Mini-Lesson 3

Fluency Goal: 120–145 words correct per minute

Remind students that...

- they can use punctuation cues to help group words into phrases.
- they should group words into phrases based on meaning.
- they should read every word accurately and at a natural pace.

Guide Practice

Introduce the story "The Water Park" on p. 72. Have students follow along as you model reading the first paragraph. Then have students read the next three sentences silently before reading them aloud with you.

If... students have difficulty recognizing punctuation cues for phrasing,
then... point out sentences with internal punctuation, such as commas and quotation marks, and model how to read each using appropriate phrasing.

On Their Own Group students to do a reading performance of "The Water Park." Assign one student to be the narrator and different students to read what each character says. Give groups time to read their parts silently. Then have each group read the story aloud to the class. Students who are not performing should track the print as they listen.

For optimal fluency, students should reread three to four times. Listen to students read and provide corrective feedback regarding their fluency and decoding.

For additional practice, use "Victor and Alma Go Exploring" on p. 73.

Fluency Lesson 13

Expression/Intonation/Characterization 1

Objectives:
- Read with expression so the passage comes alive.

MATERIALS

Worktext pp. 74–79
Routine Cards 2, 8
Leveled Reader Database

Set the scene Introduce expression to students. Today we're going to practice reading with expression, or feeling, in our voices. When we read a character's words, we should also read with expression. We can think about who the character is and then read in a way that character would talk. We can change our voices for different characters. When we read with expression, we make the story come alive.

Model and teach Introduce the passage "The Clever Squirrel" on p. 74. Remind students to speak with expression when they read the story. Show excitement or surprise when you read an exclamation mark. Adjust your voice to match the characters' feelings. This will help you understand the story and make it more interesting.

- Prepare students to follow along as you read the first two sentences aloud.
- Remind students that reading the sentences silently before reading aloud will help them become familiar with the words. Before I read aloud, I will read the sentences silently to myself. Pause to read to yourself.

Have students follow along as you model reading the first two sentences in a monotone. Then read them again expressively. Ask students which reading was more interesting and why.

Check comprehension Why does the squirrel collect food? (The squirrel is saving food for winter.)

Fluency Goal: 20–45 words correct per minute

Remind students that…
- they can read with feeling in their voices to make the story more interesting.
- they should read characters' words the way the characters would say them.
- they should read every word in the passage correctly and not skip any words.

Guide Practice

Discuss "The Clever Squirrel" on p. 74. Before having students read the next two sentences aloud with you, give them time to read the sentences silently. Continue in this way for the remaining sentences.

If… students cannot read a word,
then… have them blend decodable words **(Routine Card 2)** or say and spell high-frequency words **(Routine Card 8)**.

On Their Own Prepare the group for a choral reading of "The Clever Squirrel." You are going to read the story aloud as a group. As you read, make sure that you read with feeling to hold your listeners' attention.

Routine	Choral Reading
1. Read Together	Have students read aloud with you.
2. Reread	Then have students read aloud without you. For optimal fluency, students should reread three to four times.
3. Provide Feedback	Listen to students read and provide corrective feedback.

If students read the passage fluently, provide additional practice by assigning "Not Quite Ready" on p. 75.

Fluency Goal: 40–65 words correct per minute

Remind students that...

- they can show feeling in their voices as they read to make the story more interesting.
- quotation marks around words show that a character is speaking.
- they should read every word accurately and at a natural rate.

Guide Practice

Introduce "The Move" on p. 76. Have students follow along silently as you model reading the first paragraph. Pay special attention to reading expressively. Before having students read the next paragraph aloud, ask them to read the paragraph silently.

If... students are not reading with expression,
then... first read the fourth paragraph aloud without expression. Read it a second time with expression. Ask students to tell which reading was more interesting and why. Model expressive reading again and have students repeat until they can read the paragraph with appropriate expression.

On Their Own Pair students to do an oral reading of "The Move."

Routine	**Paired Reading**
1. Reader 1 Begins	Reader 1 reads the story to Reader 2.
2. Reader 2 Begins	Reader 2 reads the story to Reader 1.
3. Reread	For optimal fluency, students should reread three to four times.
4. Provide Feedback	Listen to students read and provide corrective feedback. Point out any words students skip over or read incorrectly.

For additional practice, have students read "Harry Says He's Sorry" on p. 77.

Mini-Lesson 3

Fluency Goal: 60–85 words correct per minute

Remind students that...

- they can show feeling with their voices to make the reading more interesting.
- they can adjust their voices to reflect different characters and what each character is feeling.
- exclamation marks signal strong feelings, such as excitement or surprise.

Guide Practice

Introduce the story "A Rainbow at Night" on p. 78. Remind students to try to read each character's words the way the character would say them. Model reading the first paragraph expressively. Then give students time to read the paragraph silently and read it aloud with them.

If... students have difficulty adjusting their voices for dialogue,
then... ask them to read the fifth paragraph silently. Discuss how Alisa is feeling. Model reading the paragraph with expression. Then ask students to repeat the paragraph aloud until they can read it fluently.

On Their Own Pair students to do an oral reading of "A Rainbow at Night."

Routine	**Paired Reading**
1. Reader 1 Begins	Reader 1 reads the story to Reader 2.
2. Reader 2 Begins	Reader 2 reads the story to Reader 1.
3. Reread	For optimal fluency, students should reread three to four times.
4. Provide Feedback	Listen to students read and provide corrective feedback regarding their fluency and decoding.

For additional practice, use "Looking at the Moon and Stars" on p. 79.

Fluency Lesson 14

Expression/Intonation/Characterization 2

Objectives:

- Read with intonation, making your voice go up and down like natural speech.

MATERIALS

Worktext pp. 80–85
Routine Cards 2, 8
Leveled Reader Database

Set the scene Explain intonation to students. Today we're going to practice intonation. When we read, our voices should rise and fall as we speak, just the way I'm talking to you right now. These changes in pitch and volume help stress the most important words, which should sound just a bit louder.

Model and teach Introduce the story "The Dog Wash" on p. 80. Discuss the use of capitalization and italics for emphasis with students. When you see a word in all capital letters or italic type, the author is telling the reader that this word is important. Speak these words louder. All capital letters and italic type tell the reader to emphasize those words.

- Remind students that reading silently before they read aloud will help them become familiar with the words. Model this skill by pausing to read to yourself.
- Tell students that you will read the first paragraph aloud. You will adjust the pitch and volume of your voice to show feeling as you read. When you read a word in italics or all capital letters, you will speak a bit louder to emphasize it.

Have students follow along as you model reading the first paragraph in a monotone. Then read it again using intonation. Ask students which reading they preferred and why.

Check comprehension Where do the students wash the dogs? (They wash the dogs in the school parking lot.)

Mini-Lesson 1

Fluency Goal: 80–105 words correct per minute

Remind students that…

- using intonation means adjusting the rise and fall of their voices as they read.
- using intonation means adjusting the volume and pitch of their voices to emphasize important words.

Guide Practice

Discuss "The Dog Wash" on p. 80. Before having students read the next two sentences aloud with you, have them read the sentences silently. Continue in this way for the remaining sentences. Check that students adjust their pitch and volume to help convey the emotion and meaning in the story.

If… students cannot read a word,
then… have them blend decodable words **(Routine Card 2)** or say and spell high-frequency words **(Routine Card 8)**.

On Their Own Prepare the group for a choral reading of "The Dog Wash." You are going to read the story aloud as a group. As you read, make sure that you read with intonation, making your voice rise and fall like natural speech.

Routine	Choral Reading
1. Read Together	Have students read aloud with you.
2. Reread	Then have students read aloud without you. For optimal fluency, students should reread three to four times.
3. Provide Feedback	Listen to students read and provide corrective feedback.

If students read the passage fluently, provide additional practice by assigning "The Search" on p. 81.

Mini-lesson 2

Fluency Goal: 100–125 words correct per minute

Remind students that...

- they should adjust the rise and fall of their voices as they read.
- they should adjust the volume and pitch of their voices to emphasize important words.
- they can adjust their voices to match the emotion and meaning of the text.

Guide Practice

Introduce the story "Police Horse" on p. 82. Ask students what they know about horses. Explain terms that they may be unfamiliar with. Have students follow along silently as you model reading the first paragraph with intonation. Give students time to read the next paragraph silently before they read it aloud with you.

If... students are not reading with appropriate intonation,

then... read the third paragraph in a monotone. Discuss how this reading doesn't sound like natural speech. Then model reading the paragraph correctly and have students repeat until they match your reading.

On Their Own Pair students to do an oral reading of "Police Horse."

Routine	Paired Reading
1. Reader 1 Begins	Reader 1 reads the story to Reader 2.
2. Reader 2 Begins	Reader 2 reads the story to Reader 1.
3. Reread	For optimal fluency, students should reread three to four times.
4. Provide Feedback	Listen to students read and provide corrective feedback.

For additional practice, use "Do Not Open Until June!" on p. 83.

Mini-lesson 3

Fluency Goal: 120–145 words correct per minute

Remind students that...

- they should adjust the volume and pitch of their voices as they read.
- they should adjust their voices to reflect the emotion and meaning of the text.

Guide Practice

Introduce "The Faces on the Mountain" on p. 84. Have students follow along silently as you model reading the first paragraph with appropriate intonation. Before having students read the next paragraph with you, have them read the paragraph silently.

If... students use intonation without regard to the meaning of the text,

then... point out different parts of the text and the feelings or meaning that each part conveys. Model how to adjust one's voice accordingly, such as lowering pitch to read serious or sad parts.

On Their Own Pair students to do an oral reading of "The Faces on the Mountain."

Routine	Paired Reading
1. Reader 1 Begins	Reader 1 reads the story to Reader 2.
2. Reader 2 Begins	Reader 2 reads the story to Reader 1.
3. Reread	For optimal fluency, students should reread three to four times.
4. Provide Feedback	Listen to students read and provide corrective feedback regarding their fluency and intonation.

For additional practice, use "The View Through Blanca's Camera" on p. 85.

Fluency Lesson 15
Expression/Intonation/Characterization 3

Objectives:
- Read dialogue in the way that the characters would say it.
- Read with expression to make the story come alive.

MATERIALS

Worktext pp. 86–91
Leveled Reader Database

Set the scene Review expression and focus on characterization. Good readers adjust their voices for different characters in the story. They also change their voices to reflect characters' changing moods and feelings. Today we will practice reading expressively and adjusting our voices to bring the characters to life.

Model and teach Introduce the reading passage "Too Hot!" on p. 86. Point out quotation marks in the story and remind students that quotation marks show dialogue, or the exact words a character says. Then discuss how all people have different voices. As they read the story, have students think about each character's mood and feelings. Explain that students should try to show those feelings in their voices when they read each character's words aloud.
- Before I read aloud, I will read the paragraph silently to myself. This helps me become familiar with the words. Pause to read to yourself.
- Then tell students that you will read the first paragraph aloud. Explain that you will look for clues about each character because you want to read the words in quotation marks the way each character would say them. Adjust your voice to reflect the character, as well as his or her mood and feelings.

Guide students to understand that characterization makes their reading more interesting and easier to understand.

Check comprehension How will Adam cool down? (He will run through the sprinkler.)

Fluency Goal: 20–45 words correct per minute
Remind students that…
- they should read each character's words the way the character would say them.
- quotation marks show dialogue, or the words a character is speaking.

Guide Practice
Discuss the story "Too Hot!" on p. 86. Before having students read the next paragraph aloud with you, have them read it silently. Then read the paragraph aloud together.

If… students have trouble recognizing dialogue, **then…** show them examples of dialogue inside quotation marks. Then have them underline any dialogue on their own copies prior to reading the text aloud.

On Their Own Prepare the group for a choral reading of "Too Hot!" You are going to read the story aloud as a group. As you read, make sure that you read each character's words in the way that you think that character would say them.

Routine	Choral Reading
1. Read Together	Have students read aloud with you.
2. Reread	Then have students read aloud without you. For optimal fluency, students should reread three to four times.
3. Provide	Listen to students read and provide corrective feedback. Check that students read with characterization and point out any words students skip or read incorrectly.

If students read the passage fluently, provide additional practice by assigning "Class Trip" on p. 87.

Mini-Lesson 2

Fluency Goal: 40–65 words correct per minute
Remind students that...

- they should read each character's words the way the character would say them.
- quotation marks show dialogue, or the words a character is speaking.
- exclamation marks show strong feeling, such as excitement or surprise.

Guide Practice
Introduce the story "A Fancy Dinner" on p. 88. Explain that *pommes frites* is a French term for fried potatoes. Have students follow along silently as you model reading the first two paragraphs with characterization. Before having students read the next paragraph aloud, have them read the paragraph silently.

If... students are having difficulty with the concept of characterization,
then... read the last sentence without expression or characterization. Ask students if this reading sounds the way the character is feeling. Then model an expressive reading and ask again. Have students repeat.

On Their Own Pair students to do an oral reading of "A Fancy Dinner."

Routine	**Paired Reading**
1. Reader 1 Begins	Reader 1 reads the story to Reader 2.
2. Reader 2 Begins	Reader 2 reads the story to Reader 1.
3. Reread	For optimal fluency, students should reread three to four times.
4. Provide Feedback	Listen to students read and provide corrective feedback.

Provide additional practice by having students read "The Car Show" on p. 89 with a partner.

Mini-Lesson 3

Fluency Goal: 60–85 words correct per minute
Remind students that...

- they should read each character's words the way the character would say them.
- quotation marks show dialogue, or the words a character is speaking.
- reading expressively and with characterization makes the story more interesting for the listener.

Guide Practice
Introduce the story "The Lost Dog" on p. 90. Have students follow along silently as you model reading the first paragraph. Before students read the next paragraph aloud with you, give them time to read it silently.

If... students have difficulty adjusting their voices to read dialogue,
then... discuss how the different characters might sound, reread the last two paragraphs, and discuss why you characterized your voice as you did for each character.

On Their Own Pair students to do an oral reading of "The Lost Dog."

Routine	**Paired Reading**
1. Reader 1 Begins	Reader 1 reads the story to Reader 2.
2. Reader 2 Begins	Reader 2 reads the story to Reader 1.
3. Reread	For optimal fluency, students should reread three to four times.
4. Provide Feedback	Listen to students read and provide corrective feedback regarding their fluency in general and their characterization and expression in particular.

For additional practice, use "Sports Day" on p. 91.

Fluency Lesson 16

Expression/Intonation/Characterization 4

Objectives:

- Read with expression so the passage comes alive.
- Adjust volume and pitch to reflect the feelings and mood of the passage.
- Read dialogue in the way that the characters would say it.

MATERIALS

Worktext pp. 92–97
Routine Cards 2, 8
Leveled Reader Database

Set the scene Review expression, intonation, and characterization with students. Remind them that they should adjust their voices to better understand and enjoy the story and to make the reading come alive for listeners.

Model and teach Introduce the story "Ethan Makes a Choice" on p. 92. Remind students that there are several ways they can make a story sound more interesting and natural. They should read with feeling and change their volume and tone to emphasize important words. They should also give each character a distinct voice that shows that character's feelings. For example, make sure that you use a different voice for Ethan and his father.

- Before you read aloud, tell students that you will read the paragraphs silently. This helps me become familiar with the words. Pause to read to yourself.
- Then tell students that you will read the first two paragraphs aloud. I will look for clues about each character because I want to read the words in quotation marks the way I think each character would say them.

Have students follow along as you model reading the two paragraphs.

Check comprehension What happens in "Ethan Makes a Choice"? (Ethan is excited about watching the fireworks. His father warns him that firecrackers are dangerous. Ethan finds a firecracker on the ground and gives it to his father.)

Fluency Goal: 80–105 words correct per minute

Remind students that…

- reading with expression makes reading sound more interesting.
- varying volume and tone makes their reading sound more natural.
- they should read each character's words the way they think the character would say them.

Guide Practice

Continue modeling expression in the story "Ethan Makes a Choice" on p. 92. Before having students read the next two paragraphs aloud with you, give them time to read silently.

If... students cannot read a word,
then... have them blend decodable words **(Routine Card 2)** or say and spell high-frequency words **(Routine Card 8).**

On Their Own Prepare the group for a choral reading of "Ethan Makes a Choice." You are going to read the story aloud as a group. As you read, make sure that you show expression.

Routine	Choral Reading
1. Read Together	Have students read aloud with you.
2. Reread	Then have students read aloud without you. For optimal fluency, students should reread three to four times.
3. Provide Feedback	Listen to students read and provide corrective feedback. Point out any words students skip over or read incorrectly. Check that they show appropriate expression as they read.

If students read the passage fluently, provide additional practice by assigning "New School" on p. 93.

Fluency Goal: 100–125 words correct per minute

Remind students that…

- they can adjust their volume and tone to emphasize important words.
- they should vary their volume and pitch to match the meaning and feeling of the passage.
- they should read each character's words as they think the character would say them.

Guide Practice

Introduce "A New Book and a New Friend" on p. 94. Before having students read the first paragraph aloud, have them read the paragraph silently. Continue in this way for the remaining paragraphs.

If… students have difficulty reading with correct expression,

then… model the following sentence: Carrie searched the new books section and found ONE remaining copy!

Ask students which words sounded a bit louder than others. (Carrie, ONE, copy) Have students echo read three or four times.

On Their Own Pair students to do an oral reading of "A New Book and a New Friend."

Routine	Paired Reading
1. Reader 1 Begins	Reader 1 reads the story to Reader 2.
2. Reader 2 Begins	Reader 2 reads the story to Reader 1.
3. Reread	For optimal fluency, students should reread three to four times.
4. Provide Feedback	Listen to students read and provide corrective feedback. Point out any words students skip over or read incorrectly. Check that they read with appropriate expression.

For additional practice, use "Chinese New Year" on p. 95.

Mini-Lesson 3

Fluency Goal: 120–145 words correct per minute

Remind students that…

- they should vary their volume and pitch to match the meaning and feeling of the passage.
- they should read dialogue in a way that shows a character's distinct voice and feelings.

Guide Practice

Introduce the story "Grandpa's Tall Tale" on p. 96. Have students follow along silently as you model reading the first paragraph with expression. Tell students to read the next two paragraphs silently. Then have them read them aloud with you.

If… students have difficulty reading with characterization,

then… explain that words near dialogue often give clues about how characters' voices should sound. Details about a character's feelings, as well as punctuation cues such as exclamation marks, show how dialogue should be read. Model relevant dialogue, and have students repeat after you.

On Their Own Group students to do a reading performance of "Grandpa's Tall Tale." Assign one student to be the narrator and different students to read what the characters say.

Routine	Paired Reading
1. Read Silently	Students read their parts silently.
2. Read Together	Each reader performs his or her assigned part.
3. Reread	Students should track the print as they listen. For optimal fluency, students should reread three to four times.
4. Provide Feedback	Listen to students read and provide corrective feedback regarding their fluency and decoding.

For additional practice, use "Clean Up!" on p. 97.

Fluency Lesson 17
Fluency 1

Objectives:
- Read text quickly, accurately, and with expression.
- Group words into meaningful phrases when reading.

MATERIALS
Worktext pp. 98–103
Routine Cards 2, 8
Leveled Reader Database

Set the scene Review fluency with students. Today we will put reading skills together. We will practice reading all the words correctly and at the speed we use when talking. We'll practice reading with expression, so the story and characters come alive. We'll also practice intonation. Intonation is the way our voices rise and fall in volume and tone as we read, just as our voices do when we talk.

Model and teach Introduce "Berry Picking" on p. 98. Today we'll read a story called "Berry Picking." After you have finished reading, I will ask you a question about what you read. As you read, remember to show feeling in your voice. Think about the meaning of the text and show what characters are feeling. This will make the story more interesting for your listeners.
- Tell students that reading sentences silently before reading aloud will help them become familiar with words. Model by pausing to read to yourself.
- Then explain that you will read the first two sentences aloud without mistakes. I will read at the same rate I use when I talk. I will read with expression and put a lot of feeling into my voice.

Have students follow along silently as you read the first two sentences without making mistakes, with expression, and at a natural rate.

Check comprehension Where does Brendan put his blueberries? (Brendan puts some blueberries in his basket and others in his mouth.)

Fluency Goal: 20–45 words correct per minute
Remind students that...
- they should read every word in the passage correctly and read at a normal pace.
- varying their volume and tone will make their reading sound more natural.
- reading expressively means showing feeling in their reading.

Guide Practice
Discuss "Berry Picking" on p. 98. Tell students to read the next two sentences silently. Then read them aloud with students, modeling a fluent reading.

If... students cannot read a word,
then... have them blend decodable words **(Routine Card 2)** or say and spell high-frequency words **(Routine Card 8)**.

On Their Own Prepare the group for a choral reading of "Berry Picking." You are going to read the story aloud as a group. As you read, make sure that you show expression and make the story interesting. Make sure that you read every word accurately. Read at the same rate you would use when talking to a friend.

Routine	Choral Reading
1. Read Together	Have students read aloud with you.
2. Reread	Then have students read aloud without you. For optimal fluency, students should reread three to four times.
3. Provide Feedback	Listen to students read and provide corrective feedback.

For additional practice, use "Train Ride" on p. 99.

Mini-Lesson 2

Fluency Goal: 40–65 words correct per minute

Remind students that...

- they should read words accurately and at a natural rate.
- varying volume and tone makes the story more interesting.

Guide Practice

Introduce the story "The Big Shot!" on p. 100. Write the following words on the board: *dribbled, huddled, baseline,* and *tipped.* Pronounce each word and have students repeat after you. Check that students know the meaning of the words. Ask students to read the first paragraph silently. Then read it aloud with them.

If... students substitute a word,
then... point to the word, sound it out, and read it correctly. Then model the sentence and have students repeat after you.

On Their Own Pair students to do an oral reading of "The Big Shot!"

Routine	**Paired Reading**
1. Reader 1 Begins	Reader 1 reads the story to Reader 2.
2. Reader 2 Begins	Reader 2 reads the story to Reader 1.
3. Reread	For optimal fluency, students should reread three to four times.
4. Provide Feedback	Listen to students read and provide corrective feedback.

For additional practice, use "Best Friends" on p. 101.

Mini-Lesson 3

Fluency Goal: 60–85 words correct per minute

Remind students that...

- they should read accurately and at a natural rate.
- using intonation means letting their voices rise and fall like natural speech.
- they should group words into meaningful phrases instead of reading word by word.

Guide Practice

Introduce "Robots" on p. 102. Then review intonation and phrasing with students. Remind them that emphasizing important words by adjusting their tone and volume makes reading more interesting for the listener. Grouping words into phrases that make sense makes their reading easier to understand. Before having students read the first paragraph with you, give them time to read the paragraph silently. Model reading fluently as they read with you.

If... students cannot read fluently without you,
then... have them finish reading the passage with you before they read in pairs.

On Their Own Pair students to do an oral reading of "Robots."

Routine	**Paired Reading**
1. Reader 1 Begins	Reader 1 reads the passage to Reader 2.
2. Reader 2 Begins	Reader 2 reads the passage to Reader 1.
3. Reread	For optimal fluency, students should reread three to four times.
4. Provide Feedback	Listen to students read and provide corrective feedback regarding their fluency.

For additional practice, use "A Class Garden" on p. 103.

Fluency Lesson 18

Fluency 2

Objectives:

- Read text accurately and at a natural pace.
- Read with appropriate phrasing and expression.

MATERIALS

Worktext pp. 104–109

Leveled Reader Database

Set the scene Review the main fluency concepts with students. Today we will practice reading all the words in a passage correctly while we read at a speed like natural speech. We will also practice grouping words and reading with expression. By practicing these skills, you will become more fluent readers.

Model and teach Introduce the story "The Queen Who Wished for Gold" on p. 104. Remind students that they should show the characters' feelings when they read dialogue. How does the queen feel at the beginning of the story? How do her feelings change in the middle and at the end? Adjust your voice to show these feelings as you read aloud.

- Remind students that reading the story silently first will help them understand what they read. Model by reading the first paragraph to yourself.
- I will read the first paragraph aloud. I will try to read every word correctly without skipping words. I will take care not to read too fast or too slow. I will also read each character's words in a way that shows what I think the character is feeling.

Have students follow along silently as you model reading the first paragraph. First read the paragraph too fast, pausing in the wrong places or speaking in a monotone. Ask students what was wrong with your reading. Repeat with no mistakes. Read in a natural tone of voice and use your voice expressively. Discuss how much clearer the second reading was.

Check comprehension What happened to the queen's dog? (She turned it into gold.)

Fluency Goal: 80–105 words correct per minute

Remind students that...

- they should read every word in the passage correctly and at a natural rate.
- grouping words into meaningful phrases will make the reading easier to understand and sound more natural.
- using expression and characterization will make their reading more interesting.

Guide Practice

Continue reading "The Queen Who Wished for Gold" on p. 104. Before students read the second paragraph aloud with you, give them a few minutes to read silently.

If... students read word by word,
then... remind them to group related words together into phrases as they read.

On Their Own Prepare the group for a choral reading of "The Queen Who Wished for Gold." You are going to read the story aloud as a group. Read words accurately and group them in ways that make sense. Read at the same rate you would use when talking to a friend.

Routine	Choral Reading
1. Read Together	Have students read aloud with you.
2. Reread	Then have students read aloud without you. For optimal fluency, students should reread three to four times.
3. Provide Feedback	Listen to students read and provide corrective feedback.

If students read the passage fluently, provide additional practice by assigning "Miguel's Pen Pal" on p. 105.

Fluency Goal: 100–125 words correct per minute

Remind students that...

- they should read every word accurately and at a natural rate.
- showing expression with their voices will make the story more interesting.
- grouping words into phrases that make sense will help listeners understand the story.

Guide Practice

Introduce the story "Isabel's Allowance" on p. 106. Before having students read the first paragraph aloud, let them read the paragraph silently. Then model reading the paragraph. First, read too slowly or read word by word. Discuss how you might improve your reading. Then model a fluent reading. Finally, read aloud with students.

If... students are skipping over or substituting words,

then... ask them to track the print as you model selected text. Then have them echo read without tracking.

On Their Own Pair students to do an oral reading of "Isabel's Allowance."

Routine	Paired Reading
1. Reader 1 Begins	Reader 1 reads the story to Reader 2.
2. Reader 2 Begins	Reader 2 reads the story to Reader 1.
3. Reread	For optimal fluency, students should reread three to four times.
4. Provide Feedback	Listen to students read and provide corrective feedback. Point out any words students skip over or read incorrectly. Check that they read with appropriate phrasing and expression and read at a natural rate.

Provide additional practice by having students read "The Envelope, Please" on p. 107 with a partner.

Mini-Lesson 3

Fluency Goal: 120–145 words correct per minute

Remind students that...

- they should read accurately and at a natural rate.
- grouping words into phrases that make sense will make their reading easier to understand.
- reading with appropriate expression, intonation, and characterization will make the passage come alive for listeners.

Guide Practice

Introduce the story "The Champion Driver" on p. 108. Have students follow along as you model reading the first paragraph, paying attention to accuracy, rate, expression, and phrasing. Give a distinct voice to the announcer. Before having students read the next paragraph aloud with you, have them read the paragraph silently.

If... students have trouble reading with appropriate expression without you,

then... model reading each paragraph with appropriate expression and have students echo read.

On Their Own Pair students to do an oral reading of "The Champion Driver."

Routine	Paired Reading
1. Reader 1 Begins	Reader 1 reads the story to Reader 2.
2. Reader 2 Begins	Reader 2 reads the story to Reader 1.
3. Reread	For optimal fluency, students should reread three to four times.
4. Provide Feedback	Listen to students read and provide corrective feedback regarding their fluency and decoding.

For additional practice, use "Band Class" on p. 109.

Fluency Lesson 19
Fluency 3

Objectives:

- Read text accurately, at an appropriate rate.
- Read text with appropriate phrasing, intonation, and expression.

MATERIALS

Worktext pp. 110–115
Routine Cards 2, 8
Leveled Reader Database

Set the scene Review the different fluency skills with students. Today we will practice reading a story with expression, so it sounds interesting to listeners. To make sure listeners understand what is happening, we will read every word correctly and not read too fast or too slow. We will group words into phrases that make sense. As you practice these reading skills, you will find that reading aloud becomes easier and more fun.

Model and teach Introduce the passage on p. 110. Today we'll read a story called "Wesley's Cast." Check that students understand that a cast is something put around broken bones to help them heal. After you finish reading, I will ask you about what you read.

- Before I read it aloud, I will read the first paragraph to myself. This helps me learn new words. Pause to read to yourself.
- Then tell students that you will read the paragraph aloud. I want to read without making any mistakes and group words into phrases that make sense. I will read with feeling to make the story interesting.

Have students follow along silently as you model reading the first paragraph at a natural rate, with appropriate phrasing and expression.

Check comprehension How did Wesley break his arm? (Wesley fell off his bike.)

Fluency Goal: 20–45 words correct per minute

Remind students that…

- they should read every word in the passage correctly and at a natural rate.
- they should group words into phrases based on meaning and punctuation cues.
- they should adjust the pitch, tone, and volume of their voices to read with appropriate expression and intonation.

Guide Practice

Have students read the next paragraph of "Wesley's Cast" on p. 110 silently before they read it aloud with you. Point out any problems with rate, phrasing, or expression. Then reread difficult sentences aloud, having students echo read.

If… students cannot read a word, **then…** have them blend decodable words **(Routine Card 2)** or say and spell high-frequency words **(Routine Card 8).**

On Their Own Prepare the group for a choral reading of "Wesley's Cast." You are going to read the story aloud as a group. As you read, make sure to read the words accurately and at a natural rate. Group words instead of reading word by word, and read with feeling.

Routine	**Choral Reading**
1. Read Together	Have students read aloud with you.
2. Reread	Then have students read aloud without you. For optimal fluency, students should reread three to four times.
3. Provide Feedback	Listen to students read and provide corrective feedback.

If students read the passage fluently, provide additional practice by assigning "Fresh Paint" on p. 111.

Mini-Lesson 2

Fluency Goal: 40–65 words correct per minute

Remind students that...

- they should read every word accurately and at a natural rate.
- they can adjust their voices to show feeling and make the story more interesting.
- they can adjust their voices to stress important words.

Guide Practice

Introduce the story "The Big Storm" on p. 112. Then review intonation. By changing your tone and volume, you can emphasize words. Have students read the first paragraph silently. Model a fluent reading. Then have students read the paragraph aloud.

If... students skip or substitute a word,
then... point to the word, sound it out, and read it correctly. Then model reading the entire sentence, and have students repeat it after you.

On Their Own Pair students to do an oral reading of "The Big Storm."

Routine	Paired Reading
1. Reader 1 Begins	Reader 1 reads the passage to Reader 2.
2. Reader 2 Begins	Reader 2 reads the passage to Reader 1.
3. Reread	For optimal fluency, students should reread three to four times.
4. Provide Feedback	Listen to students read and provide corrective feedback. Point out any words students skip over or read incorrectly.

Provide additional practice by having students read "Meteor Shower" on p. 113 with a partner.

Mini-Lesson 3

Fluency Goal: 60–85 words correct per minute

Remind students that...

- they should read accurately, not skipping or substituting any words.
- reading with feeling will make the story more interesting.
- they should group words in phrases that make sense.

Guide Practice

Introduce the story "Street Fair" on p. 114. Have students follow along as you model reading the first paragraph, paying attention to accuracy, rate, expression, and phrasing. Tell students to read the next paragraph silently. Then have them read aloud with you.

If... students have difficulty reading with appropriate expression,
then... read the second paragraph in a monotone and then expressively, and ask which reading was more interesting and easier to understand. Model reading the paragraph again and have students repeat it after you.

On Their Own Pair students to do an oral reading of "Street Fair."

Routine	Paired Reading
1. Reader 1 Begins	Reader 1 reads the story to Reader 2.
2. Reader 2 Begins	Reader 2 reads the story to Reader 1.
3. Reread	For optimal fluency, students should reread three to four times.
4. Provide Feedback	Listen to students read and provide corrective feedback regarding their fluency and decoding.

For additional practice, use "Snowman" on p. 115.

Fluency Lesson 20
Fluency 4

Objectives:
- Read text fluently and accurately.
- Read with appropriate rate, phrasing, and expression.

MATERIALS
Worktext pp. 116–121
Routine Cards 2, 8
Leveled Reader Database

Set the scene Review fluency with students. You've practiced many reading skills. Today we'll practice reading all the words correctly and at a natural rate like regular speech. We'll practice intonation, or the way our voices rise and fall naturally as we speak or read. We'll also read with expression, reading characters' words to show how we think the characters would say them.

Model and teach Introduce the passage "The Monster Under the Bed" on p. 116. After you finish reading, I will ask you about what you read.

Tell students that reading fluently will allow them to show the meaning in what they read rather than simply reading word by word.

- Tell students they should read the paragraph silently before they read it aloud. This will help them learn the words. Then model by pausing to read to yourself.
- Then tell students that you are going to read the first paragraph aloud. You will read without making any mistakes and at a natural speed. I will let the volume and pitch of my voice rise and fall naturally. I will group words in a way that makes sense and read with feeling.

Have students follow along silently as you model reading the first paragraph.

Check comprehension Tell me what the story is about in two to three sentences. (Anna thinks there is a monster under her bed. Sara comes into the room to check. Sara finds their cat under the bed.)

Mini-Lesson 1

Fluency Goal: 80–105 words correct per minute

Remind students that…
- they should read every word in the passage correctly and at a natural rate.
- reading silently to themselves will help them become familiar with the words.
- their voices should go up and down like when they are talking to someone.

Guide Practice
Continue modeling fluency with "The Monster Under the Bed" on p. 116. Before having students read the next paragraph aloud with you, have them read the paragraph silently. Then read the first sentence of the paragraph aloud, modeling a fluent reading.

If… students cannot read a word,
then… have them blend decodable words **(Routine Card 2)** or say and spell high-frequency words **(Routine Card 8).**

On Their Own Prepare the group for a choral reading of "The Monster Under the Bed." You are going to read the story aloud as a group. As you read, remember to read accurately, at a speed like normal speech, and with expression.

Routine	**Choral Reading**
1. Read Together	Have students read aloud with you.
2. Reread	Then have students read aloud without you. For optimal fluency, students should reread three to four times.
3. Provide Feedback	Listen to students read and provide corrective feedback.

If students read the passage fluently, provide additional practice by assigning "The Lady Next Door" on p. 117.

Mini-Lesson 2

Fluency Goal: 100–125 words correct per minute

Remind students that…

- they should read every word accurately at a natural rate.
- showing expression with their voices makes their reading more interesting.
- using punctuation cues can help them group words in phrases that sound natural and make sense.

Guide Practice

Introduce "Do Animals Know?" on p. 118. Then model a reading with poor phrasing while students follow along silently. Ask students whether or not your reading was easy to understand and why. Then model appropriate phrasing and have students read the paragraph aloud.

If… students are not pausing for commas, **then…** make sure they can identify commas by asking them to point out commas in the passage. Model a paragraph two or three times and have students read with you until they can read it fluently.

On Their Own Pair students to do an oral reading of "Do Animals Know?"

Routine	**Paired Reading**
1. Reader 1 Begins	Reader 1 reads the passage to Reader 2.
2. Reader 2 Begins	Reader 2 reads the passage to Reader 1.
3. Reread	For optimal fluency, students should reread three to four times.
4. Provide provide **Feedback**	Listen to students read and corrective feedback. Point out any words students skip over or read incorrectly.

Provide additional practice by having students read "At Splendid Shore" on p. 119 with a partner.

Mini-Lesson 3

Fluency Goal: 120–145 words correct per minute

Remind students that…

- they should read words accurately and at a natural rate.
- they should group words in phrases that make sense.
- reading with expression makes the story sound more natural and interesting.

Guide Practice

Introduce the story "Bad Day" on p. 120. Have students follow along as you model the first paragraph, paying attention to accuracy, rate, expression, and phrasing. Before having students read the next paragraph aloud with you, have them read the paragraph silently.

If… students have trouble reading fluently without you, **then…** have them read a passage with you multiple times, focusing on particular skills they struggle with, before reading with a partner.

On Their Own Group students to do a reading performance of "Bad Day." Assign one student to be the narrator and different students to read what the characters say.

Routine	**Reading Performance**
1. Read Silently	Students read their parts silently.
2. Read Together	Each reader performs his or her assigned part.
3. Reread	Students should track the print as they listen. For optimal fluency, students should reread three to four times.
4. Provide Feedback	Listen to students read and provide corrective feedback regarding their fluency and decoding.

For additional practice, use "Trains" on p. 121.

Fluency Student Worktext

Name ______________________________

Up All Night

Adrian only wanted one thing for his birthday. "I want to stay 12
up all night!" Adrian said. 17

"Are you sure?" asked Adrian's mother. "All night is a very 28
long time." 30

Adrian nodded. "I will not fall asleep," he said. 39

Adrian asked his friend Marco to spend the night. The boys 50
ate pizza and cake. They played games and watched movies. 60

When Adrian's mother got up in the morning, she saw the boys. 72
They were fast asleep. 76

School + Home **Directions** Read the story aloud with your child two or three times. Then have your child practice reading the story to you. Remind your child to read every word and not skip any words.

Name ______________________________

Melissa's New Room

Melissa moved into a new house. Melissa has a new room. 11
Melissa's mother asked her to help pick out things for her 22
new room. 24

Melissa and her mother went shopping. They saw a lot of 35
cool things. Melissa was not sure what she wanted. 44

Then Melissa saw a lamp. It was a big red flower. It was 57
very tall! Melissa liked the lamp. 63

Soon Melissa had a red and white room. The blankets had 74
flowers on them. The big flower lamp was in the corner. 85

School + Home **Directions** Read the story "Melissa's New Room" aloud to your child. Then have your child practice reading the story with you until he or she can read it without making mistakes.

Name ________________________________

Canada

Have you ever been to Canada? Canada is the country north of the 13
United States. Instead of 50 states, Canada has ten provinces and 24
three territories. It became a country in 1931. 32

Canada is the second largest country in the world! Canada is more 44
than 4,600 miles wide from the Pacific Ocean in the west to the 57
Atlantic Ocean in the east. It has big mountain ranges, prairies, and 69
tundra. Canada has many rivers and lakes too. 77

Canada is a big country, but it only has about 32 million people. 90
Most of those people live within 100 miles of the U.S. border. 102

School + Home **Directions** Read the passage to your child once. Then read it together two or three times. Make sure that your child reads each word accurately.

Name ___________________________

Penguins

Penguins are interesting animals. You may have seen them in a 11
movie or in a zoo, but you won't see one walking down the street! 25

There are 17 different kinds of penguins. Some of these kinds are 37
king, emperor, fairy, and rockhopper. Penguins live in Africa, South 47
America, Australia, and Antarctica. Most penguins live on islands, 56
but some penguins live on the coasts of continents. Most penguins 67
live in large groups called *colonies.* 73

Penguins are birds. They have feathers, and they lay eggs. Penguins 84
are different from most other birds in one major way. Penguins 95
don't fly! They don't need to fly because they swim. Penguins swim 107
in the ocean to find the fish that they eat, and they can swim very fast! 123

Directions Take turns reading the story "Penguins" aloud with your child. Read the story at least two or three times. Remind your child not to skip any words. Make sure your child pronounces each word correctly.

Name ____________________

Dad's Train

Fridays are Ivan's favorite day of the week. Every Friday, Ivan and 12
his mom pick up his dad at the train station. 22

Ivan's dad rides the train to work every day. He works very far away, 36
but the train is fast. His dad likes riding the train because he can read a 52
book or watch a movie. Sometimes his dad calls home and talks to Ivan 66
while the train rolls down the track. 73

On Fridays, Ivan and his mother go to the train station. They wait 86
on the platform. Ivan can see the train from a long way away. It has 101
a very bright light on the front. 108

When the train pulls into the station, Ivan's dad gets off the train. 121
Ivan's family leaves the station and goes to Ivan's favorite pizza 132
place. They order a big pizza, and they have dinner together. 143

School + Home **Directions** Read the story to your child, and then read it together two or three times. Then ask your child to read the story to you without skipping any words or making any mistakes.

Name ____________________

Best Friends

Omar and Ravi live next door to each other in an apartment building. 13
They have known each other since they were babies. Omar and Ravi 25
are best friends. 28

On school days, Omar knocks on Ravi's door at 7:30. He and Ravi 41
take the elevator downstairs with Omar's mom. Then they wait outside 52
for the school bus. The boys ride the bus together, play on the 65
playground with their other friends, and go inside when the bell rings. 77

Omar and Ravi are in the third grade. They are both in Mr. Berry's 91
class. Omar's favorite subject is math, but Ravi's favorite subject 101
is social studies. They both love to play sports at recess. Their favorite 114
sport is kickball. 117

After school, the boys take the school bus home to their apartment 129
building. They take the elevator upstairs to Omar's apartment. Then 139
Omar's mom makes them a snack, and they do their homework together. 151

Later Ravi goes home for dinner. The boys will see each other in 164
the morning. 166

School + Home **Directions** Take turns reading the story aloud with your child. Then have your child practice reading it without skipping any words. Make sure your child pronounces each word correctly.

Name ______________________________

Look Both Ways

Alicia and her little sister Sandy are walking to school. It is cold. 13
Sandy wants to get inside fast. Sandy steps into the street. 24

"Stop!" Alicia says. She pulls Sandy out of the street. 34

"Why?" Sandy asks. "I am cold. I want to walk fast!" 45

"Sandy, we must be careful. We look both ways before we walk 57
in the street," Alicia says. 62

"I looked!" Sandy says. 66

Alicia shakes her head. "No, you did not. You must be careful," 78
she says. 80

"Why?" Sandy asks again. It is very cold outside. Alicia shivers 91
in her coat. She puts her hands in her pockets. 101

"Cars drive fast. They cannot stop if you walk in front of them," 114
Alicia says. "You need to be safe. Try again. Look both ways 126
this time." 128

Sandy looks right. There are no cars. She looks left. A red car 141
drives by. It goes very fast! Sandy waits until it is gone. "Now 154
can I walk?" she asks. 159

"Yes, you can walk. Now it is safe," Alicia says. 169

School + Home **Directions** Read the story aloud with your child two or three times. Then have your child practice reading the story to you. Remind your child to read every word and not skip any words.

Name ____________________

Election Day

"Wake up! Today is Election Day. We need to go vote," Devon's 12
mother says. 14

Devon gets up and gets dressed. He has a special pin to wear. Today 28
is a very important day. People will pick the country's president today. 40

Devon cannot vote. He is not old enough. You have to be 18 to vote. 55

Devon goes to school with his mother before class. People are voting 67
there. He waits while she votes. Devon is proud. 76

More people come to vote. Devon's mother helps them. "Just fill in 88
the circles with your pen," she says. 95

Devon helps too. When people are done, he takes their pens. Then 107
he gives the people a sticker. "I voted!" the sticker says. 118

Then Devon goes to class. "I helped people vote," he tells his teacher. 131

"You did a good job, Devon," his teacher says. 140

Devon's class has an election too. They learn about voting. 150

After school, Devon helps again. He gives out many stickers. 160
It is a long day, but Devon is happy to help. Voting is important. 174

Directions Read the story "Election Day" aloud to your child. Then have your child practice reading the story with you until he or she can read it without making mistakes.

Name ______________________________

The New Player

Max and his neighborhood friends were playing basketball at the park, just 12
like they did every Saturday. 17

“You’re getting REALLY good, Max,” Omar called as Max shot another 28
basket. Max knew he was playing better, but he still had a LOT to learn to 44
play like Ruben Jones. Ruben was Max’s favorite high school player. 55

A while later, Max noticed a boy about their age watching very closely 68
from behind the court’s fence. 73

“Who’s that kid in the wheelchair?” Max whispered, turning toward Omar. 84

Just then, the boy called out as he wheeled onto the court, “Hey, can 98
I play?” 100

“Well, CAN you play?” Omar asked in a surprised voice. 110

“Sure I can!” the boy laughed. “I’m Calvin Jones, and I’m visiting my 123
cousin Ruben this week. I learned to play from him, and I might teach 137
you guys a few things!” 142

Max stared. “Your cousin is Ruben Jones, the star of the high school 155
team? Awesome!” 157

Calvin rolled to the middle of the court. He raised the ball above his head 172
and made a perfect basket. All the boys stared. “Wow!” they cried together. 185

As they played, everyone tried to keep up with Calvin, but he was the best 200
player on the court that day. Being in a wheelchair didn’t stop him! 213

School + Home **Directions** Have your child read the story aloud with you. If your child mispronounces a word, help him or her sound it out. Ask your child to read all words correctly without substituting other words or leaving words out.

Name ____________________

What the World Has to Offer

Kaylee enjoys going for walks in the woods with her mom. She likes all the 15
different plants (except for poison ivy). She likes lots of other living things, 28
too, especially animals. She learns so many interesting things from her mom 40
during their walks. 43

"Is this one poison ivy, Mom?" Kaylee asks. She points to a green leafy 57
vine winding around the trunk of a tree. Kaylee's mom is a botanist, or a 72
scientist who studies plants. Most people call her Dr. Porter, but to Kaylee, 85
she is Mom. "No, that's a plant called Virginia creeper," Mom replies. "It 98
looks like poison ivy, but it won't cause an itchy rash like poison ivy does." 113

"Mom, did you always want to be a scientist?" Kaylee asks. 124

"Well, at first I wanted to be a ballet dancer," Mom laughs. "Then I 138
wanted to be an animal doctor, then an artist, and then a writer. I didn't 153
decide to study plants until I was in college." 162

"Wow, you changed your mind a lot!" Kaylee exclaims. 171

"Yes, I suppose I did," says Mom, smiling. "It's important to try different 184
things and explore new ideas and new interests. Changing your mind, 195
being curious, asking questions, and learning what the world has to offer 207
are all part of growing up." 213

Directions Read the story "What the World Has to Offer" aloud to your child, and then have your child read the story with you two more times. Encourage your child to read every word accurately.

Name ________________________________

A Day at Camp

Susan was excited and nervous on the first day at camp. The camp was 14
up in the mountains. It was beautiful and green. There were tall pine 27
trees and flowers everywhere. 31

Susan was staying in a little cabin with her friends. When the bus dropped 45
them off at camp, everyone put their bags in the cabins. They brought 58
sleeping bags, coats, and summer clothes to wear. 66

After they put away everything, everyone went to the camp lodge. They 78
would eat meals in the dining hall at the lodge. Some of the camp 92
counselors served lunch. They had turkey sandwiches, apples, and chips. 102

Then the camp director spoke. "Welcome to Camp Whispering Pines," 112
she said. "My name is Miss Linda. We are all going to have a fun week. 128
Do you have any questions?" 133

A girl Susan did not know raised her hand. "What is there to do here at 149
camp?" she asked. "Where are the TVs?" 156

Miss Linda laughed. "There are no TVs here. Don't worry. You will find 169
plenty to do. Today we will get to know each other. Tonight we will sing 184
camp songs around a big fire. Tomorrow you will be able to swim in the 199
lake or ride horses. There will also be arts and crafts lessons." 211

Susan raised her hand. "My dad said there were bears around the camp. 224
Was he right?" she asked. A few of the other girls looked scared. 237

Miss Linda smiled. "Don't worry about bears. Many years ago we had a 250
problem with bears. They liked to eat our food. Now that we have the 264
lodge, the bears stay away," she said. 271

School + Home **Directions** Read the story to your child, and then read it together two or three times. Then ask your child to read the story to you without skipping any words or making any mistakes.

Name ____________________

The Mystery of the Missing Balls

The bell rang for recess. Rob jumped up and walked to the door. He was 15
the first one in line. Once everyone was lined up, Mrs. James let the class 30
go outside. Rob walked as fast as he could without getting in trouble. 43

"No running in the halls!" a teacher shouted. 51

Rob slowed down a little. He was going to play dodgeball with his friends. 65
He practiced all weekend with his little brothers. Rob pushed through the 77
door and out into the warm sunshine. Rob walked over to the equipment 90
shed. Mr. Rose was waiting there to pass out balls and jump ropes. 103

"Hi, Mr. Rose. Can I have a red ball?" Rob asked. 114

"Sure, Rob. What are you playing?" Mr. Rose asked. He was the physical 127
education teacher. 129

"I am playing dodgeball with my friends," Rob said. 138

Mr. Rose opened the door of the shed. "Well, that is odd," he said. 152

Mr. Rose opened the door wide. Rob could see inside. There were no red 166
balls! "Where are the balls?" Rob asked. 173

"I do not know, Rob. Let me go check," Mr. Rose said. He walked over to 189
the school door and disappeared inside. 195

Rob waited. A small crowd formed around him. "No balls? This is not 208
fair!" Matt said. "Where did they go?" Rob could see the clock. Recess 221
was almost half over! 225

Finally, Mr. Rose came out of the school. He was dragging a big bag of 240
red balls behind him. "Some of the balls were flat, so Mr. Carr pumped 254
them up," he said. He handed a ball to Rob. Now they could play! 268

Directions Take turns reading the story aloud with your child. Then have your child practice reading it without skipping any words. Make sure your child pronounces each word correctly.

Name ____________________

The New Baby

Kevin's mother went to the hospital. She had a new baby. 11
Kevin wants to see them. Kevin's dad drives him to the hospital. 23

"Are you ready to meet the new baby?" Kevin's dad asks. 34

Kevin nods. They go into the hospital room. 42

Kevin's mother sits in her bed. She holds a tiny baby. "This 54
is your baby brother, Patrick," she says. 61

Kevin looks at Patrick. "Can I hold him?" Kevin asks. 71

"Yes," Kevin's mother says. "You are his big brother!" 80

School + Home **Directions** Read the story aloud with your child two or three times at a natural pace. Then have your child practice reading the story to you as if he or she were talking to you.

Name ______________________________

A New Trick

Lucia has a very smart dog. Her dog's name is Tiny. Tiny knows 13
a lot of tricks. He can sit and beg, and he can roll over. 27

Lucia teaches her dog a new trick! She teaches Tiny how to dance. 40
It is easy. 43

First, Lucia tells Tiny to sit. She gives the dog a treat. Tiny is 57
happy. He likes treats. 61

Then Lucia holds a treat over Tiny's head. She moves the treat in 74
a circle. Tiny spins around to watch the treat. He is dancing! 86

School + Home **Directions** Read the story aloud to your child. Then have your child practice reading the story with you until he or she can read it quickly.

Name ______________________________

Ryan Does Laundry

Ryan gets all the laundry baskets. He puts them in the 11
laundry room. Then he sorts the clothes. All the white 21
clothes go together. All the light colors go together, and 31
the dark colors go together. 36

First, Ryan puts some white clothes in the washer. He 46
only puts in enough clothes to fill the washer. He does 57
not put in too much clothes. Then he adds the soap and 69
closes the door. 72

Ryan pushes the button for whites. The washer fills 81
with water, and the clothes spin around in the water. Soon 92
they are clean. 95

When the washer is done, Ryan puts the clothes in the 106
dryer. After they are dry, he folds them and puts them in 118
the baskets. 120

School + Home **Directions** Take turns reading the story "Ryan Does Laundry" aloud with your child. Read the story at least two or three times. Remind your child not to read too fast or too slow.

Name ______________________________

Piggy Banks

“We will be learning about money this week,” Mrs. Mason said. 11
She held up a piggy bank. “Noah, will you give a pig to every 25
student?” she asked. 28

“Yes, Mrs. Mason,” Noah said. There was a box full of piggy 40
banks. There were red pigs, blue pigs, pink pigs, and green pigs. 52
Noah gave each student a pig and took a green one for himself. 65

“This week, we will learn about saving money. If you save 40 cents 78
every day, how much money will you have at the end of a month?” 92
Mrs. Mason asked. 95

Tasha answered, “Twelve dollars.” 99

“Right. Twelve dollars may not seem like much now. But if you 111
saved 40 cents a day for a whole year, you’d have 146 dollars,” 124
Mrs. Mason explained. Everyone was surprised. “We’ll talk about 133
how to save money, and we’ll have a quiz on Friday,” she said. 146

Directions Read the story to your child once, and then read it together two or three times. Make sure that your child reads at a normal rate.

Name ______________________________

Growing Watermelons

Dana and her mother planted a garden in their backyard. They 11
planted Dana's favorite food. They planted watermelons! 18

Dana planted watermelon seeds in little pots. Her mother put 28
the pots in the kitchen window. Every day, Dana looked to see 40
if the seeds were growing. One day little plants started to grow 52
in two of the pots. 57

Dana and her mother took the pots outside and planted the new 69
little plants in hills of dirt in the garden. The new plants did not 83
need a lot of water. 88

Dana took care of the plants. She checked them every day. She 100
pulled weeds when they came up. Dana kept the bugs away. 111
Soon the plants grew vines covered in flowers. 119

Some of those flowers had tiny watermelons under them. 128
Dana worked hard to keep the plants healthy. The watermelons 138
started to grow. 141

After three months, the melons are finally ready! Dana's mother 151
cuts up the melon. She gives Dana a big chunk of juicy, red fruit. 165
Dana takes a big bite. It's delicious! 172

Directions Take turns reading the story aloud with your child. Then have your child practice reading it quickly. Make sure your child does not skip words.

Name ______________________________

Carla's Big Project

Carla had been working on her science project for weeks, and now she was 14
done. Tomorrow she would present her project in front of the whole class. 27
Every time she thought about speaking in front of her class, Carla's knees 40
felt weak. 42

That night Carla did not feel like eating dinner. She just sat at the table 57
while her family talked, laughed, and ate. "What is wrong, Carla?" her 69
father asked. 71

"I'm okay," she said. 75

When he came to say goodnight, her father asked, "What's bothering you?" 87

Carla took a deep breath. "I have to show my science project to the class 102
tomorrow. I am afraid everyone will laugh at me!" 111

"Why would anyone laugh?" her father asked. 118

"What if I make mistakes?" Carla asked. 125

Her father shook his head. "Making mistakes is a part of learning. You 138
should just try to do your best." 145

The next day Carla presented her project. She made a few mistakes, but if 159
anyone noticed, at least no one laughed. 166

Directions Read the story "Carla's Big Project" aloud to your child at a natural rate. Take turns reading the parts of Carla and her father. Challenge your child to read the story as if he or she were speaking to you.

Name ____

Music Class

"We have had a lot of fun singing this year. We have snapped and 14
clapped and danced. Now we are going to start playing instruments," 25
Mr. Riley told the class. 30

Gavin raised his hand. "What kind of instruments?" he asked. 40

"Today we will try the recorder," Mr. Riley said. He pulled a box out 54
from under his desk. It was full of black and white tubes. They had 68
holes in them. 71

Mr. Riley gave one of the tubes to each student. Gavin looked at his 85
tube. It had holes all the way down the tube. It was closed at one end. 101
How could he play this? 106

Mr. Riley picked up one of the tubes. "This is a recorder. You blow 120
in this end." He blew in the closed end. The recorder made a sound. 134

"Cool!" Gavin said. 137

"It is cool," Mr. Riley said. "These holes help you make different 149
sounds." Mr. Riley put two fingers over the holes. Then he blew 161
into the recorder again. It made a different sound! 170

"Can we try that?" Gavin asked. 176

"Yes! Now you can try!" Mr. Riley said. 184

School + Home **Directions** Read the story aloud with your child two or three times at a natural pace. Then have your child practice reading the story to you as if he or she were talking to you. Remind your child to read every word and not skip any words.

Name ______________________________

Basketball Practice

Logan tried out for the basketball team. After a week, Coach Robins 12
put up a list of names of players who made the team. Logan made it! 27

Logan went to the first practice. He put on his blue uniform. All the 41
boys practiced hard as Coach Robins watched them play. 50

After practice, Coach Robins talked to Logan. "You did well!" he said. 62
"But you do need to work on your free throws." 72

"I know," Logan said. He was not very good at shooting free throws. 85
"I will practice hard!" 89

"Shoot 100 free throws every day," Coach Robins said. "Soon you will 101
get better." 103

Logan nodded. "I can do that," he said. 111

Every day after Logan came home from school, he did his homework. 123
Then he put on his basketball uniform and took his basketball outside. 135
He had a basketball hoop outside. 141

Logan had marked a free throw line on the ground. He stood behind 154
the line. He picked up a ball and lined up his shot. Logan took a deep 170
breath and shot the ball. Logan shot 100 free throws. 180

After two weeks, Coach Robins talked to Logan again. "I can tell 192
you are practicing! I am proud of you!" he said. 202

School + Home **Directions** Read the story aloud to your child. Then have your child practice reading the story with you until he or she can read it at a rate that is neither too slow nor too fast.

Name ______________________________

Be Polite, Please!

Josh's mother was always nagging him to be polite. Whatever Josh did, 12
his mom was telling him what to say and what to do. 24

"Say *please,* Josh," Mom whispered whenever Josh asked for anything. 34
"Say *thank you,*" Mom reminded Josh whenever anyone gave him 44
something. "Say *may I* and *you're welcome,* Josh," Mom called loudly 55
as he got on the school bus. 62

Josh tried to be polite, but he often forgot. He had other things to think 77
about, such as soccer. None of his friends said things like *please* and 90
thank you. Being polite just didn't seem important to Josh. 100

"Why do you want me to say *please* and *thank you,* Mom?" Josh asked 114
one afternoon. "What's so great about saying those certain words?" 124

"It's more than just the words themselves, Josh," Mom replied. "Being 135
kind and polite shows respect. Using polite phrases lets people know that 147
you respect them and intend to treat them well. Good manners say a lot 161
about a person." 164

Josh thought a minute. Then he said, "I will be polite from now on. 178
I want good manners to say a lot about me too!" 189

School + Home **Directions** Read the story to your child once, and then read it together two or three times. Make sure that your child reads at a normal rate.

Name ______________________________

George Washington

George Washington was the first president of the United States. His 11
face is on the quarter and on dollar bills. 20

Washington was born on February 22, 1732, in Virginia. At the time, 32
Virginia was a British colony. Washington did not go to school much 44
but mostly taught himself. His early years were not always happy. 55
Washington's father died when he was eleven years old. 64

When Washington grew up, he joined the Virginia Militia. He led 75
soldiers north to deliver an important message. People from France 85
were moving into land claimed by Britain. Washington asked them to 96
leave, but the French people refused. This started a war! Washington 107
fought in the war, which the British won. 115

In 1758, Washington was elected to Virginia's government. At this point, 126
the colonists were angry. Britain was charging them many taxes to pay 138
for the war. The colonists did not think this was fair. 149

In 1776, the colonies declared independence. War broke out and lasted 160
five years. The colonies won and were now free. During the war, 172
Washington helped to create a new government for America. 181

In 1789, Washington became the first president of the United States. 192
He was elected again three years later. People tried to elect him again, 205
but Washington said no. He went back to his home in Virginia, where 218
he died in 1799. 222

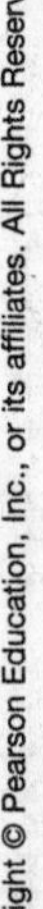

Directions Take turns reading the story aloud with your child. Read the story at least two or three times. Remind your child not to read too fast or too slow and to pause briefly when he or she sees a comma.

Name ____________________

Cynthia Rylant: A Writer's Story

Cynthia Rylant loves to write. She writes picture books, nonfiction, and 11
poetry books. Her books are in thousands of libraries and bookstores. 22
How did she become an author? How does she work? 32

Cynthia Rylant was born in 1954. She grew up in the mountains of West 46
Virginia. As a young girl, Cynthia had very few books to read, so she spent 61
hours by herself. She played and walked. "I loved everything about life," 73
she said. As she grew older, Cynthia thought about her future. Maybe she 86
would be a teacher or a nurse. 93

After college, Cynthia worked in a library and discovered children's books. 104
Two of the ones she loved were *The Animal Family* and *The Ox-Cart Man.* 118
She read them over and over. Then she began to write her own stories. 132

When Cynthia was twenty-five, her first book was published. It was *When* 144
I Was Young in the Mountains. It is a book about growing up in West 159
Virginia. Now Cynthia was an author! 165

Since then, Cynthia has written more than 100 books. She writes novels, 177
stories, and poems. Many of her books have won awards. 187

What is Cynthia's recipe for writing a good book? She starts with her 200
imagination. "You have to sit quietly, clear your mind, and wait," she says. 213
Next, she creates an interesting plot and sprinkles it with details. That is 226
how her books start. 230

Cynthia now lives in Oregon, where her days are calm and simple. "That 243
way," she explains, "I'm ready to sit down and write when it's time." 256

Directions Read the story aloud to your child at a natural rate. Challenge your child to read the story as if he or she were speaking to you.

Name ____________________

Ramon's Book

One day Ramon's teacher, Mr. Martin, had a great idea. "Tomorrow we 12
are going to visit Mrs. George's kindergarten class. You will read to the 25
children," Mr. Martin said. 29

Ramon raised his hand. "Mr. Martin, what will we read?" he asked. 41

"That is a good question! I would like each of you to bring a book to read. 58
Pick a book you loved when you were in kindergarten," Mr. Martin said. 71

Ramon thought about this all day. Which book should he bring? When 83
Ramon got home, he looked at all the books on his bookshelf. He had 97
lots of stories about animals and adventures, but none of them seemed 109
right. Ramon was still thinking about it at dinner. "What is wrong?" 121
Ramon's mother asked. 124

"We are reading to little kids tomorrow. I do not know which book to 138
bring," Ramon said. He was starting to worry. What if he could not 151
find a book? 154

Ramon's mother smiled. "We read all the time when you were little. 166
Do you remember your favorite book?" she asked. 174

"No. I looked at all my books, and I could not find anything," 187
Ramon said. 189

"I have just what you need," Ramon's mother said. She got up and left the 204
kitchen. Ramon listened as she walked up the stairs and into her room. 217

A minute later she was back. She held a book in her hands. "Why don't 232
you read this one?" she asked. She handed him the book. 243

Ramon smiled. It was *Where the Wild Things Are.* "This is perfect, Mom. 256
Thank you!" he said. 260

School + Home **Directions** Take turns reading the story aloud with your child. Then have your child practice reading it quickly. Make sure your child does not skip words.

Name ______________________________

The Big Tree

There is a big tree in Joel's backyard. It has strong branches. 12

Joel likes to climb it. 17

"Be careful!" says Mom. "Do not climb too high!" 26

"I will be careful, Mom," Joel says. 33

Joel starts to climb. He reaches up and jumps. He 43
pulls himself up. He climbs from branch to branch. 52

Joel can see the ground below. It is not far below, but 64
climbing is fun! 67

School + Home **Directions** Read the story aloud to your child. Then have your child practice reading the story with you until he or she can read it at a rate that resembles natural speech.

Name ______________________________

Ouch!

Amanda fell off her bike and cut her knee. 9

Amanda put her bike away. She looked for her mother. 19
"Mom! I got hurt," she said. 25

Amanda's mother was in the kitchen. "Oh no!" Mom said. 35
"Let's clean that up." 39

Mom got out a washcloth and cleaned the cut. "That will 50
feel better now," Mom said. 55

Amanda said, "That didn't hurt much." Then she went to get 66
on her bike again. 70

School + Home **Directions** Read the story aloud with your child two or three times at a natural pace. Then have your child practice reading the story to you as if he or she were talking to you. Remind your child to read every word and not skip any words.

Name ______________________________

A Day at the Amusement Park

Every summer Chris's mother and father take him to the 10
amusement park. They spend all day at the park. They play 21
games and go on the rides. 27

Chris loves roller coasters. He wants to ride them all day. 38
Chris loves everything about roller coasters. He loves the 47
slow ride up the first hill. He loves looking down the hill 59
too. He even likes picking up speed as he plunges down 70
at top speed. Chris's favorite part is going upside down 80
in loops. 82

Afterward, they go home. Chris can't wait to come back again! 93

School + Home **Directions** Read the story to your child once, and then read it together two or three times. Make sure that your child reads at a normal rate.

Name ____

Mount Rushmore

Every year two million people flock to a mountain in South Dakota 12
Why do they come? They come to see Mount Rushmore. 22

Mount Rushmore is more than just a mountain. There are four stone 34
faces carved into the side of the mountain. The faces are four presidents: 47
George Washington, Thomas Jefferson, Theodore Roosevelt, and 54
Abraham Lincoln. The carved faces are 60 feet tall! 63

It took a long time for sculptors to carve the faces into the mountain. 77
More than 400 workers spent fourteen years carving the mountain. 87

Now visitors come from all over to see the presidents' faces on 99
Mount Rushmore. 101

Directions Take turns reading the story aloud with your child. Read the story at least two or three times. Remind your child not to skip any words and not to read too fast or too slow.

Name ____________________

The Mystery of the Disappearing Friends

Trisha wants to play volleyball with her friends. She wonders, "Where 11
are they?" Trisha goes to Pam's house. She knocks on the door. 23

"Hello, Trisha," says Pam's mother. "Pam is not home. Sorry." 33

Trisha goes to Kelly's house. She rings the doorbell. 42

Kelly's brother answers the door. "Kelly is not here," he tells her and 55
shuts the door. 58

Now Trisha is getting mad! Where are all of her friends? She turns and 72
walks home. Trisha is sad. 77

When Trisha gets home, she looks unhappy. Trisha's mother notices 87
and asks, "What is wrong?" 92

"My friends are off somewhere playing without me!" Trisha says. 102
"I just wanted to play volleyball with them." 110

"Well, why don't you look for them? Maybe they are at the volleyball 123
court already," Trisha's mother says. 128

"Okay, maybe you are right," Trisha says. She takes her volleyball and 140
walks down the street to the park. As she gets close to the court, she sees 156
her friends! 158

"Trisha, where were you? Come play with us!" they say. 168

School + Home **Directions** Take turns reading the story aloud with your child. Then have your child practice reading it at a natural pace. Make sure your child does not skip any words.

Name ____________________

Double Trouble!

"I'll race you to the car!" Maya yelled to her twin brother, Jamar. Maya and 15
her family were going to see Grandma. 22

Jamar scrambled into the seat, shoving Maya from behind. "Hurry up!" 33
he said. 35

"Kids," Dad sighed, slamming the car door. "You're not going to fight the 48
whole way to Grandma's. What did I tell you?" 57

"Be on your best behavior," Maya and Jamar said together. This started a 70
wave of laughter. Within seconds, they were fighting and shouting at each 82
other again. 84

Mom turned and gave them a warning look, which stopped the fighting for 97
the rest of the trip. 102

Finally, they arrived at Grandma's house. "There's trouble!" she exclaimed. 112

"Why do you say trouble?" Maya asked, surprised. 120

"You two remind me of how your Aunt Kay and I got into trouble when 135
we were little," Grandma said. "We were twins, too, you know. I know 148
the double trouble twins can get into!" 155

Maya wrinkled her nose, and Jamar rolled his eyes. Then the whole family 168
burst out laughing! 171

School + Home **Directions** Read the story aloud to your child at a natural rate. Challenge your child to read the story with no mistakes as if he or she were speaking to you.

Name ____________________

The Last Day of School

Today is the last day of school, so Jesse is excited. There is no more 15
work to do. He is also sad. He will miss his friends. He will miss 30
his teacher, Mr. Burns. 34

Today is a fun day. First, Mr. Burns reads to the class. He reads a 49
book about pirates. Mr. Burns wears a pirate hat. He has a toy 62
bird. The kids laugh at Mr. Burns. He laughs too. 72

Then they play games. Mr. Burns breaks the class into teams. 83
Each team has four students. Then Mr. Burns asks them questions. 94
If someone knows the answer, he rings a bell. Each answer wins a 107
point for that team. 111

The questions are fun. They are about things the class learned. Jesse 123
answers a question about weather, but his team does not win. 134
Everyone gets a prize. 138

Then it is party time! The kids eat lots of food. Then Mr. Burns 152
says goodbye to everyone. All of them are ready for summer. It was a 166
good year. 168

School + Home **Directions** Read the story aloud with your child two or three times at a natural pace. Then have your child practice reading the story to you as if he or she were talking to you. Remind your child to read every word and not skip any words.

Name ______________________________

The Princess and the Frog

One day a princess was playing in the woods. She threw a ball up into 15
the air and caught it again. Then the ball hit a tree. The ball bounced 30
away. Far away, she heard a splash. The princess followed the sound 42
until she found a pond. Her ball was at the bottom of the pond. "Oh no! 58
What will I do?" the princess said. 65

"I could get it for you," a voice said. 74

The princess looked around. A frog sat by the edge of the pond. 87
"You can talk?" she asked. She had heard stories about talking frogs. 99
They were often princes. 103

"Of course I can talk!" the frog said. "Would you like your ball?" 116

"Yes, please," the princess said. She gave the frog a smile. 127

"What will you give me?" the frog asked. 135

In the stories, the princess kisses the frog. "I will give you a kiss," 149
she said. 151

The frog hopped into the pond. It swam to the ball and brought it 165
back to the princess. 169

The princess kissed the frog. Nothing happened. 176

"I am not a prince. I am just a talking frog," the frog said. 190

Directions Read the story aloud to your child. Then have your child practice reading the story with you until he or she can read it at a natural pace without errors.

Name ____

Into the Darkness

Tina was excited to be babysitting alone. She had babysat before, but her 13
older sister had always come along. Tonight Tina was on her own, just 26
like an adult. 29

After reading bedtime stories and saying goodnight to the twins, Tina went 41
downstairs to watch television. As she turned on her favorite show, the TV 54
shut off, and the house went dark. 61

"What's going on?" Tina whispered. For a moment she sat still, afraid to 74
move. Then she got up slowly and went to the telephone. She called the 88
number Mrs. Green had given her. 94

"Mrs. Green? It's Tina," she said. "The power went off." Mrs. Green 106
explained where the electric box was in the basement and how to turn the 120
lights back on. 123

From the top of the steps, the dark basement looked like a cave. Tina got 138
up her courage, took a breath, and then walked slowly down the stairs into 152
the darkness. She felt blindly and then found the electric box exactly where 165
Mrs. Green said it would be. When she flipped the electric switch, all the 179
lights came on at once. 184

As she walked up the steps and into the light, Tina felt more grown up 199
than ever! 201

School + Home **Directions** Read the story "Into the Darkness" aloud with your child two or three times. Encourage your child to read at an appropriate rate. Challenge your child to read the story without making any mistakes.

Name ____

Nathan the Great

Aaron's older brother, Nathan, seemed to be good at everything. Nathan 11
was the best soccer player on the team. He played all positions well. Nathan 25
was a remarkable basketball player. He could even shoot baskets with his 37
eyes closed! For the third year in a row, Nathan was the star quarterback 51
on his school's football team. Nathan got A's in all his classes, and he even 66
helped younger students with math. 71

Aaron loved and admired Nathan, but he felt discouraged. "I just wish 83
I was as good as you at something," Aaron complained. 93

"Come on, Aaron," Nathan said. "You're only ten years old! I'm sixteen, 105
so I've had six more years to study, learn, and practice. When I was your 120
age, I wasn't very good at anything!" 127

"Really?" Aaron gasped in surprise. "You were bad at something once?" 138

Nathan laughed. "I was terrible at almost everything, but I didn't let that 151
bother me. Instead, I watched the older kids play sports, I copied their 164
moves, and I just kept practicing. If I didn't understand something, I 176
asked questions." 178

"You mean if I practice, I could be as good as you at sports?" Aaron 193
asked hopefully. 195

"You'll probably be even better!" Nathan exclaimed. "Now let's go play 206
some ball!" 208

School + Home **Directions** Read the story aloud with your child. Encourage your child to read at a natural pace.

Name ______________________________

Birthday Cake

Today is a special day for Tim and Peter. It is their mother's birthday. The 15
boys want to give her a gift. They will make a cake! The boys' dad will 31
help. Tim likes yellow cake, but Peter likes chocolate. They agree to make 44
a yellow cake with chocolate frosting. 50

The boys get out a bowl and spoon. They use a box of cake mix. Tim pours 67
mix into the bowl while Peter reads the box. 76

"We need two eggs," Peter says. He gets the eggs and cracks them into the 91
bowl. Peter is careful not to get shells in the bowl. 102

Tim stirs in the eggs. "What else do we need?" he asks. 114

Peter reads the box. "Water and oil," he says. Peter gets a measuring cup. 128
He carefully measures the water and pours it into the bowl. 139

While Tim stirs, Peter gets the oil. Peter pours the oil into the cup. Then he 155
pours it into the bowl. Tim stirs it all together. "This smells delicious!" 168
Tim says. 170

Peter pours everything into a cake pan. The boys' dad puts the pan in the 185
oven to cook for half an hour. Then he takes it out to cool. 199

When the cake is cool, the boys put chocolate frosting on it. Next, they 213
decorate it with candles. Now it is ready for Mom! 223

After dinner, the boys are excited to give Mom their gift. "Are you 236
ready for dessert?" Tim asks, smiling. 242

"You made dessert? I can't wait to see it!" Mom says. 253

Dad lights the candles. Then they bring the cake in and all sing to Mom. 268
She blows out the candles. "Thank you so much!" she says. 279

Directions Take turns reading the story aloud with your child. Then have your child practice reading it at a natural pace. Make sure he or she does not skip any words.

Name ____________________

The Reading Contest

Ellie's class is having a reading contest! Who will read the most books? 13
Ellie wants to win. 17

The three kids who read the most will win prizes. Third prize is a gift 32
card for books. Second prize is two movie tickets and a book. First prize 46
is a boxed set of books. 52

Ellie really wants to win. It should be easy because she loves to read. 66
But another student named Gabe also loves to read. 75

Gabe reads a lot of comic books. They are shorter than the books Ellie 89
reads. She does not think it is fair for comic books to count as books. 104

On the first day of the contest, Ellie's teacher, Mr. Hall, reads the rules. 118
Instead of counting books, they will count pages. Kids who read long 130
books will have a chance to win too. 138

Now Ellie is happy because she knows she can win! Every night, Ellie 151
reads. On the bus, Ellie reads. She tries to read during dinner, but her 165
mother makes her stop. She says reading at the table is not polite. 178

The contest lasts the whole month. Finally, it is over. Ellie has read a 192
lot of books, but Gabe read a lot of books too. 203

Mr. Hall throws the class a party to celebrate all their reading. He 216
tells them that they read more than any class he's ever taught. Then 229
he gets out the prizes. Who will win? Ellie is excited. 240

Ellie gets first prize! Gabe wins the second prize. 249

School + Home **Directions** Read the story aloud to your child at a natural rate. Challenge your child to read the story with no mistakes as if he or she were speaking to you.

Name ______________________________

The Broken Plates

"Dinner is almost ready!" Mom says. "Please set the table." 10

Salim puts down his game. He walks into the kitchen and gets plates. 23

As he walks to the table, Salim's dog runs in front of him. "Oh, no!" 38
he says. Salim trips and falls. The plates go flying! 48

CRASH! The plates break on the floor. 55

Mom turns around. She sees the broken plates. "It is all right, Salim. 68
Let's clean it up together." 73

Directions Read the story aloud with your child two or three times at a natural pace. Then have your child practice reading the story to you as if he or she were talking to you. Remind him or her to read every word and not skip any words.

Name ____________________

Car Trip

Shawn is bored. He is sitting in the back seat of the car. Shawn's 14
family has been driving all day! 20

"I am BORED!" Shawn says. 25

"Me too!" says Shawn's sister, Wendy. 31

"I know a game you can play," says Mom. 40

"What is it?" Shawn asks. He is tired of looking at farms along 53
the road. 55

"You can find cars from different states. I will list all the states 68
for you. Then you cross them out when you see a car from there," 82
Mom says. 84

"Thank you!" Shawn says. 88

School + Home **Directions** Read the story aloud to your child. Then have your child practice reading the story with you until he or she can read it quickly.

Name ______________________________

Bowling

"Did you bring shoes?" Dee asks. Dee and her friends are going 12
bowling! 13

"I don't have bowling shoes, so I will rent them," Kim says. 25

"We brought ours," says Joan. "We brought balls too." She and her 37
sister Karen bowl all the time. They belong to a bowling league. 49

Dee and Kim rent shoes and find balls. They all go to their lane 63
to put on shoes. Then they are ready to bowl! 73

Joan goes first and gets a strike! Joan is an excellent bowler. 85

Kim goes next and hits six pins. Kim gets to try again. This 98
time she hits two pins. 103

Dee doesn't hit any pins, so she tries again and hits four. 115

Karen hits seven pins and then hits the other three. She gets a spare! 129

School + Home **Directions** Read the story "Bowling" aloud with your child two or three times. Encourage your child to read at a natural pace. Challenge him or her to read the story without making any mistakes.

Name ___________________________________

Aunt Carrie

Alice admires her aunt. Aunt Carrie is a doctor. She saves people's 12
lives every day. 15

Carrie works in the emergency room in a big hospital downtown. 26
She works at night because people get hurt at night too. She works 39
with lots of other doctors and nurses to take care of patients. They are 53
people who come to the hospital for help. 61

Carrie helps all kinds of people. She takes care of little children who 74
get sick or fall off their bikes. She also takes care of adults who have 89
fevers or coughs or other illnesses. 95

Carrie also takes care of people who have accidents. Sometimes people 106
fall down and break bones. Other people fall off their bikes or get into 120
car accidents. Carrie takes care of all of them. 129

School + Home **Directions** Read the story aloud with your child. Encourage your child to read every word at a natural pace.

Name ______________________________

The Catch

"No one is EVER going to hit a ball over here," Ben said. Ben and 15
his dad were sitting out in left field. Ben had brought his glove to 29
the game hoping to catch a ball. 36

"Don't say that," Dad said. "You never know what will happen. 47
Aren't you having fun?" 51

Ben looked down. He was wearing a new jersey and his favorite 63
baseball glove. He had been wearing the glove since batting 73
practice before the game. Ben also had a big cup of soda in his cup 88
holder. The floor under his seat was covered in peanut shells. He had 101
been eating them since the game began. "I guess this has been fun," 114
he said. 116

CRACK! Ben looked up. A ball was flying directly at them. Ben 128
jumped up and held his glove high in the air. The ball flew right into 143
his glove! He had made the catch! 150

School + Home **Directions** Read the story aloud to your child in a way that sounds natural. Then ask him or her to read the story to you, focusing on reading at a good pace. Challenge your child to read without making any mistakes.

Name ______________________________

Paul the Painter

It was very early in the morning. The first golden rays of the sun 14
spilled over the mountains, filling the valley below with warmth 24
and light. 26

Paul smiled, picking up his box of brushes and paints. He loved 38
living in the mountains. He enjoyed the quiet beauty of the forest. 50
Well, at least it was quiet MOST of the time (the crows were really 64
noisy sometimes). 66

Walking along the forest path, Paul came to his favorite place to 78
paint. He set out his paints, brushes, and canvas. Then he thought 90
about what he would paint (this was always the hardest part). 101

Paul decided to paint a beautiful yellow tree. First, he mixed white, 113
grey, and brown paints for the trunk. Then he mixed some bright 125
yellow for the leaves. 129

Paul began painting, dipping his brush first into a jar of water and 142
then into the paints on his tray. With tiny strokes of color, Paul brought 156
the tree to life on his canvas. 163

Directions Take turns reading the story aloud with your child. Then have him or her practice reading it at a natural pace. Make sure your child does not skip any words.

Name ______________________________

Take a Hike!

"Hurry up, Mom!" Sasha says. She runs along the path. Sasha and 12
her mom are walking up a path to the top of a hill. You can see the 29
woods and the lake from the top. 36

"Be careful!" Mom says. "This is not a race!" Mom carries a bag 49
with food for their lunch. She does not walk as fast as Sasha. 62

Sasha is too excited to slow down. "Will we be able to see the 76
camp?" she asks. Sasha is glad to spend some time alone with Mom. 89

"Yes, I think so," Mom says. 95

"Will we see our house?" Sasha asks. She stops to pick some 107
yellow flowers. They smell sweet. 112

Mom laughs. "No, Sasha. We live very far away," she says. 123

Sasha starts up the path again. This time she skips. They are almost 136
to the top. At the end of the path, there is a picnic area. There are 152
shady trees and picnic tables. Two families are sitting there eating 163
lunch. 164

"Wow, Mom, look!" Sasha says, pointing. From the picnic area, 174
she can see the woods below them. At the bottom of the hill, the 188
blue lake sparkles. 191

School + Home **Directions** Read the story to your child at a natural speaking rate. Then ask your child to read the story without reading too fast or too slow. Encourage him or her not to skip or substitute any words.

Name ______________________________

Weather

"Today we will talk about something new," Maggie's teacher, 9
Mr. Root, said. "We will learn about weather." 17

Maggie raised her hand. "Mr. Root, we know about weather. 27
Today is sunny. That is weather," she said. 35

Mr. Root nodded. "Yes, that is one kind of weather. There are 47
many more kinds too," he said. Mr. Root went to the board. 59
"Can someone else tell me about kinds of weather?" he asked. 70

Bobby raised his hand. "Rain!" he said. 77

"Good!" Mr. Root said, and he wrote it on the board. "What 89
other kinds are there?" he asked. 95

Mary raised her hand. "Snow!" 100

"Yes, and what else?" Mr. Root asked as he wrote it down. 112

The students were quiet for a moment. Greg raised his hand. 123
"I know! I know! Hail," he said. 130

"Yes, Greg. That's right," Mr. Root said. 137

Greg smiled with pride. 141

"We will start with these," Mr. Root said. "Let's talk about 152
what weather is. Weather is what happens up in the sky. 163
Sometimes there are no clouds. Those are sunny days. 172
Sometimes there are clouds. Clouds can make rain, snow, 181
and hail. Wind moves the clouds around the world." 190

School + Home **Directions** Read "Weather" aloud to your child. Then have him or her practice reading the story aloud with you at a natural rate without making any mistakes.

Name ____________________

Sunflowers

Sunflowers are very interesting plants. They are named for their 10
big yellow flowers. Sunflowers are both beautiful and useful. 19

Sunflowers are annual plants. That means that each plant grows for only 31
one year, and then it dies. Each sunflower plant grows from a seed. 44
The plant grows one stem and digs roots deep into the ground. 56

The stem grows taller and taller. Sunflowers can grow up to 12 feet 69
tall! Leaves grow in pairs from the stem. Soon a flower bud grows 82
at the top of the stem. The bud will turn during the day to keep facing 98
the sun. Then one big flower blooms. This flower can be four to six 112
inches across. Most sunflowers are yellow, but they can be red or 124
orange too. 126

Each flower has petals around its edge and rows of tiny seeds in the 140
middle. The seeds grow and grow until they are very heavy. Then the 153
flower droops and wilts. The seeds begin to drop to the ground. New 166
plants will grow from these seeds the next year. 175

Sunflower seeds are good for more than planting. You can eat them 187
too! People use sunflower seeds to make cooking oil. They also roast 199
the seeds in ovens and eat them as snacks. Mashed sunflower seeds 211
can be spread on bread like peanut butter. 219

School + Home **Directions** Read the story to your child accurately at a natural speaking rate. Then ask your child to read the story aloud accurately and without reading too fast or too slow.

Name ______________________________

The Greatest Soccer Player You Will Ever Meet

Victor's family had just moved to a new neighborhood, and Victor was 12
miserable. He was not eager to start all over at a new school. He missed 27
his old friends. "Why couldn't we stay at our old apartment?" Victor asked 40
sadly, even though he already understood the reasons. 48

"I know that this move has been tough for you, Victor," said his dad. He 63
put his arm around Victor's shoulders. "Trust me, things will improve." 74

A few days later, Victor's dad took him aside. "Son, I've signed you up at 89
Aim Center near the school. It's a kind of boys' club that offers a range 104
of activities. You can train for sports, take music lessons, and even 116
practice math." 118

Victor looked hopeful. "Will guys be there who like math and soccer as 131
much as I do?" 135

"You won't know unless you go!" said Victor's dad. 144

That afternoon at Aim Center, Victor stood in the entrance feeling nervous. 156
Just then, a boy about Victor's age came up behind him. "You're Victor, 169
right?" he said with a grin. "I saw that you were signed up for soccer and 185
math. I'm Gonzo, the greatest soccer player and math wiz that you will 198
ever meet!" 200

"And I'm the greatest soccer player and math wiz that *you* will ever meet!" 214
Victor said, laughing. 217

Directions Read the story aloud to your child at a natural rate. Then ask him or her to read the story back to you at a natural rate. Challenge your child to read the story without making any mistakes.

Name ______________________________

Summer's New Bicycle

Summer wanted a new bicycle. She already had a bicycle, but it was her 14
sister's. It was old and dirty. Summer wanted a shiny new bicycle like her 28
friends had. 30

"Your bicycle still works fine," Summer's mother pointed out. 39

"It's all dirty! The paint is scratched up," Summer said. She wanted a bicycle 53
just like her friend Val's. That bicycle was purple. It had a light on the front. 69

"It's not so bad," Summer's mother said. 76

Summer made a face. "It's *green,*" she said. "I don't like green." 88

Summer's mother sighed. "Okay, you can have a new bicycle," she said. 100

Summer clapped her hands and hugged her mother. "Thank you!" she 111
said happily. 113

"Don't thank me yet. You can have a new bicycle, but you have to earn it," 129
her mother said. "I will make you a list of chores and how much I will pay 146
you to do each one. You can only use the money for a bicycle. If you earn 163
enough money before school starts, we can pick out a new bicycle." 175

Summer frowned and looked at the floor. Then she looked up and said, 188
"Okay, I'll do it!" 192

The next day, Summer found the list of chores on the table. She would have 207
to do a lot of chores to earn the bicycle! 217

Summer worked hard. She washed the car, pulled weeds, and helped do the 230
laundry. Every time she finished a job, her mother crossed it off the list. 244
Then she added the money to Summer's total. Finally, right before school 256
started, Summer had earned enough money. 262

"Are you ready to buy your bicycle?" Summer's mother asked. 272

"Yes!" Summer said. 275

School + Home **Directions** Read the story to your child at a natural rate. Then challenge your child to read the story aloud at a natural rate without making any mistakes.

Name ___________________________

Zoo Trip

"I want to see the polar bears first," Marcus said. 10

"I want to see the tigers first," Danny said. The boys were sitting on the bus. 26
Their class was on a field trip. Today they were going to the zoo! 40

They had studied different animals all month. Mrs. Wolf told them all sorts 53
of interesting facts. "Polar bear babies are all twins," Marcus said. "They 65
live up north in very cold places." 72

"Every tiger has different stripes," Danny said. "They like to swim, too!" 84
Tigers were his favorite animal. They were large and powerful. They had a 97
really loud roar. 100

When the bus got to the zoo, the students lined up and followed Mrs. Wolf. 115
A tour guide showed them around. They saw polar bears and penguins. 127
They saw tigers and elephants. 132

The class ate lunch in the zoo's butterfly garden. Then one of the 145
zookeepers showed them a big red and green parrot. Her name was Rosie, 158
and she talked! 161

After lunch, the class broke into smaller groups. Marcus and Danny 172
decided to go with the group visiting the Australian animals. 182

"Australia has neat animals!" Marcus said. "They have lots of them here." 194

Their guide brought them to a fence looking down on a space with lots 208
of grass. Kangaroos hopped around in the grass. "Their babies are called 220
joeys. They live in their mother's pouch when they are little," Danny said. 233

"Do you have wombats here?" Marcus asked the guide. 242

"Yes, we do. They live in that building over there," the guide said. 255

Marcus and Danny had a great day at the zoo! 265

School + Home **Directions** Take turns reading the story aloud with your child. Read the story at least two or three times at a natural rate. Then challenge your child to read without making any mistakes.

Name ____________________

Blue's Bubble Bath

Ruby's dog Blue was afraid of water. She did not swim. She did 13
not go near lakes. She did not even like the rain. One day, Blue 27
got away. When Ruby found her, Blue was covered in mud. 38

Ruby filled up the bath, but Blue jumped out. Ruby did not know 51
what to do. Then she had an idea. She poured bubbles in the water. 65
The bubbles hid the water. When Blue saw the bubbles, she chased 77
them. She jumped right in the bath! Blue was not afraid at all. Ruby 91
cleaned her in no time. 96

School + Home **Directions** Read the story to your child. Then ask your child to read the story aloud, pausing for punctuation and grouping words instead of reading word by word.

Name ______________________________

Spelling Bee

"May, your word is *clutch*," Mrs. Horn said. 8

May was nervous. She and Michelle were the last two left in 20
the spelling bee. "Could you use it in a sentence?" she asked. 32

"When it's windy, I clutch my bag tightly," Mrs. Horn said. 43

"*Clutch*," May said. Then she spelled it. 50

"That is right," Mrs. Horn said. She turned to Michelle. 60
"Michelle, your word is *feast*." 65

Michelle thought for a moment. Then she spelled the word. 75

"I am sorry, Michelle. That is incorrect. May, you win!" 85
Mrs. Horn said. 88

School + Home **Directions** Read "Spelling Bee" to your child. Then have your child practice reading the story with you, pausing for punctuation and grouping words together so they make sense.

Name ______________________________

Ice Cream

It was a very hot day, and Alonso and Pablo wanted a cool treat. "Mom, 15
can we have some ice cream?" Alonso asked. 23

"We don't have any ice cream. Would you like to make some?" 35
Mom asked. 37

"How do we make it?" Pablo asked. 44

"First, I will mix milk and sugar. Then I will pour it into a can, seal it 61
up tight, and put ice around it. Next, you two will roll the can around 76
until the ice cream freezes," Mom told them. 84

"Cool! We can do that!" Alonso said. 91

Mom made the mix for them. Then she put together the can. The boys 105
rolled the ice cream. At last, they ate it. It was the best ice cream they 121
had ever eaten! 124

School + Home **Directions** Read the story to your child. Then have your child read the story to you, grouping the words appropriately.

Name ____

School Shopping

"Mom, I don't like those pants at all!" Sharon protested. 10

Sharon's mother checked a list in her hands. The list had come 22
with Sharon's new class schedule. "Sharon, those pants are on your 33
list," she said. 36

"What is that list?" Sharon asked. 42

"It is a list of pieces for your school uniform," her mother said. 55

"We have to wear uniforms?" Sharon asked. 62

"Yes, you do," her mother said. 68

"Why?" Sharon asked. She had never had to wear a uniform before. 80

"The school district decided that everyone should wear the same 90
things. Then no one will wear shorts that are too short or shirts 103
with bad words on them," Mom told her. 111

"I guess if everyone has to wear them, I will too," Sharon said. 124

Directions Take turns reading the story aloud with your child. Read the story at least two or three times. Remind your child to pause briefly when he or she sees a comma and to group words instead of reading word by word.

Name ______________________________

The Yard Sale

Grumbling, Mika started throwing old toys into a box. She kept 11
stopping to take things back out. “I can’t sell my model cars,” she 24
thought. “I might want to play with them again.” 33

Mika’s family was having a yard sale tomorrow. Mika was 43
supposed to be gathering old toys to sell. 51

Soon, Mika had a pile of toys she wanted to keep. “I cannot find 65
anything I do not want! Who would buy all this stuff anyway?” 77
she sighed. 79

Mika’s mom appeared in the doorway. “Have you decided what to 90
sell?” she asked. 93

“I can’t sell any of these toys!” Mika cried. “What if I need them 107
for something?” 109

Mom looked around and smiled. “Honey, you don’t play with most 120
of these toys anymore, do you? Why not let someone else enjoy them?” 133

Mika thought about what Mom said. It was true. She had not played with 147
her model cars in years. She didn’t even have room for most of the toys in 163
her bedroom. Maybe they could make someone else happy now. Mika 174
started filling the box with toys for the yard sale. 184

School + Home **Directions** Read “The Yard Sale” aloud with your child two or three times. Make sure your child reads with correct phrasing, pausing for commas and end punctuation.

Name ______________________________

Learning to Swim

This summer Rosa is spending a whole month at camp. “I will 12
learn to swim!” she calls to her grandmother from the bus. 23

The next afternoon, Rosa’s swim class meets by the pool. Rosa 34
and her new friends climb down the ladder into the water. 45

When class begins, Rosa listens carefully to Miss Park, her 55
swimming teacher. First, Miss Park teaches the children to float 65
on their backs. Then they practice kicking their legs straight up 76
and down. Finally, they learn to pull themselves through the water 87
using their arms. 90

“Swing your left arm back and roll your head to the left,” Miss 103
Park explains. “Now, take a breath over your left shoulder. Next, 114
swing your left arm up and reach over your head. Roll your face 127
to the front and blow the air through your mouth into the water.” 140

That night Rosa writes to her grandmother. “Soon I will be a 152
great swimmer! When you visit, I will race across the pool to 164
meet you!” 166

School + Home **Directions** Read the story to your child. Then ask your child to read the story aloud, grouping words and pausing briefly for commas.

Name ____________________

One Day in the Big City

Megan's class was taking a field trip. They were going to New York 13
City. Megan had never been to a big city before. She was excited, but 27
she was also scared. 31

Megan's class got on a large bus. It was a two-hour drive, so they left 46
early in the morning. Soon they were getting off the bus in New York 60
City. "Stay with the group!" their teacher, Mr. Young, called. Megan 71
looked around. The buildings were so tall! The streets looked like 82
canyons of brick and glass. Lights flashed. The city was bright and 94
loud. Cars filled every street. There were so many people! They hurried 106
down the streets. 109

The class went to the top of the Empire State Building. When Megan 122
looked down, she felt sick. "Look how high up we are!" she said. The 136
class visited the Statue of Liberty. They had a picnic in Central Park. 149
The class had fun! At last, Megan climbed on the bus to go home. She 164
sang out, "I love New York!" 170

School + Home **Directions** Ask your child to read the story aloud, grouping the words in each sentence. If the words sound awkward, read the sentence or sentences aloud and have your child read after you, matching your phrasing. Then challenge your child to read the story without making any mistakes.

Name ____________________

The Best Brother Ever

Kevin loved his big brother, Greg. They did fun things together, 11
like climbing trees in the park. They played catch too. Kevin 22
thought Greg was the best brother in the whole world. 32

Greg was going away to school soon. Kevin was sad. He did not 45
like to think about it. He wished that Greg would stay. “Could you 58
stay near home?” Kevin asked, walking to the park with Greg. 69

“This is a very good school,” Greg said. “Going there is the 81
best thing I can do.” 86

Kevin did not understand, but he knew that Greg had to go. Why 99
was it so far away? Kevin wanted to go with him. “I will miss you 114
so much!” he told Greg. 119

“I will miss you, too, little brother,” Greg said, smiling at Kevin. 131
“But I will call you. I will be home every few weeks. I will be home 147
for holidays. Do not worry, Kevin. I will still be your big brother, no 161
matter where I go!” 165

Kevin smiled too. Greg was the best brother ever. 174

School + Home

Directions Read “The Best Brother Ever” to your child. Then have your child practice reading the story aloud with you, pausing briefly for commas and grouping words together.

Name ____________________

Naveed's Favorite Uncle

Every day after school, Naveed walks to Uncle Omar's house and waits 12
there until his mother gets off work. Uncle Omar is a carpenter, and he and 27
Naveed spend their afternoons together working on interesting projects. 36
Naveed has four uncles, but Uncle Omar is his favorite, a secret he has 50
never shared with Uncle Omar. 55

One afternoon, Uncle Omar asks, "Would you like to help me build a 68
birdhouse?" 69

"Sure!" Naveed answers excitedly. "Will we need special equipment?" 78

"No, I have the tools and materials we need," Uncle Omar replies. "We'll 91
need safety glasses, an electric saw, and a drill. They are in my workshop." 105

A few minutes later, Uncle Omar is sawing pine boards into square pieces. 118
"After we finish sawing the wood, we'll squeeze a thin layer of glue along 132
the edges. Then we'll nail the squares together to fasten the walls while the 146
glue hardens," Uncle Omar explains. "Our birdhouse will be solid!" 156

"I'll get the glue and nails. I know where you keep all your supplies!" 170
says Naveed. 172

Uncle Omar, smiling at Naveed, says, "I'm lucky that my favorite nephew 184
is such a helpful assistant!" 189

Naveed smiles back at Uncle Omar. "I am very lucky too," he says. "My 203
favorite uncle is the best carpenter and friend in the world!" 214

Directions Read "Naveed's Favorite Uncle" aloud with your child two or three times. Help your child read with appropriate phrasing by grouping words together that make sense and pausing at commas.

Name ______________________________

Which Instrument Will You Learn to Play?

Have you ever thought about learning to play a musical instrument? Your 12
school might have a great orchestra or a marching band. You might 24
join some day. First, you must make a tough decision. Which instrument 36
will you learn to play? 41

Think about which instruments you like to hear. Do you enjoy the tones of 55
the flute, or do you favor the blasts of the trumpet? Maybe the singing 69
of a violin is what you like best. 77

Aside from what you like to hear, think about how comfortable the 89
instrument would be to play. Some stringed instruments, such as the piano 101
and harp, sit on the floor. You play these with your hands and fingers. 115
Others, such as the violin, are held under the chin. You finger the upper 129
part of the strings with one hand and move a bow across the lower part of 145
the strings with the other hand. All brass instruments, such as the trumpet 158
and trombone, are played with the mouth and hands. Brass instruments 169
have mouthpieces, or special openings, that you must blow into very hard. 181
You must develop strength in your lips and cheek muscles to play their 194
loud blasts! 196

Learning to play an instrument will take years of practice. Make sure the 209
instrument you pick is one that you will enjoy playing—and practicing! 221

Directions Take turns reading the passage aloud with your child. Help your child read with correct phrasing by reminding him or her to pause for commas and group words meaningfully.

Name ______________________________

The Nature Walk

"Come on, Jacob, we're going on a nature walk with Aunt Carol!" Mom 13
called up the stairs. 17

"Oh, brother," Jacob grumbled, rolling his eyes. "What could be more 28
boring than a nature walk?" Aunt Carol was visiting them from Arizona. 40
She seemed nice enough, but she always wanted to do things outdoors. 52
Usually Jacob stayed inside whenever Aunt Carol did her outside stuff, but 64
today his mom wanted him to come along. 72

Jacob liked to play inside. He liked video games and books. He could go 86
all kinds of places in books, like to the ocean or a castle. He was really 102
good at video games too. 107

Once they were outside, Jacob noticed that the weather was really nice. 119
It was a cool October day, but the sun was shining. The colors of 133
changing leaves looked bright against the clear blue sky. 142

As they walked through the forest, Aunt Carol pointed to things on the 155
ground. "Look, there's a chipmunk stuffing its cheeks with seeds, and 166
here are some deer tracks in the mud. See the tiny mushrooms growing 179
on that old tree stump?" 184

At first, Jacob just looked at his feet as he walked. Then he stopped 198
to look where Aunt Carol was pointing. Once, he held out his 210
hand, and a beautiful butterfly landed on his fingers. 219

After about an hour, Mom suggested they go home. "But I want to look 233
around some more!" Jacob exclaimed. He liked the outdoors more than 244
he thought! 246

Directions Take turns reading "The Nature Walk" aloud with your child. Read the story at least two or three times. Remind your child to group words and pause briefly when he or she sees a comma.

Name ____________________

Making Maple Candy

Every winter my dad and I go out to the forest behind our house to 15
collect sap from maple trees. We carry heavy buckets of sap back to 28
our house, where we pour it into a huge kettle on the stove. Then we 43
boil the sap until it gets sticky and thick. It takes a long time, and it's a 60
lot of work, but it's worth it. 67

"Is it ready yet, Dad?" I ask for the tenth time. I stand near the stove 83
watching the bubbling pot. The maple syrup smells wonderful. It is 94
sweet and nutty. 97

"Not yet," Dad answers with a smile. This is part of the fun, this 111
game we play where I keep asking and Dad keeps answering. "Be 123
careful not to get too close to the stove. The syrup is very hot!" 137

Finally, it's ready! We will put some of the syrup in bottles, so we can 152
use it on pancakes and waffles later. Dad carefully pours some of the 165
hot syrup from the large kettle into a small cooking pot. 176

Then Dad carries the pot outside, and I follow him. We look for a place 191
where the snow is deep and fresh and clean. We have to work fast, 205
because it is so cold outside that the maple syrup starts to cool very 219
quickly. 220

Holding the pot by its handle, I pour the maple syrup on the snow in 235
thin ribbons. As the syrup touches the snow, it cools and hardens. At last, 249
I lift the hard ribbons of maple candy from the snow and take the first 264
delicious bite. 266

School + Home **Directions** Read "Making Maple Candy" to your child. Then have your child practice reading the story aloud, reading groups of words together in phrases that make sense. Challenge your child to read the entire story without making any mistakes.

Name ______________________________

Seeds

A man came up a hill. His name was Johnny Appleseed. 11
He had a pot for his hat, a pack on his back, and an apple 26
in his hand. 29

I ran up the hill to meet Johnny. I called his name and tapped 43
on his back. He let me peek inside his pack. It was filled 56
with seeds! 58

Johnny gave me lots of seeds. Then he helped me plant 69
them. Seeds need sun and water. These seeds will be big 80
trees! 81

School + Home **Directions** Read the story to your child. Then ask your child to read the story, making sure to group words.

Name ____________________

Mules

Mitch and Hank have a ranch with mules. Mitch has 10
Patch, and Hank has Fetch. 15

"Patch and Fetch are fine mules," said Mitch. "But which 25
mule is stronger?" 28

Mitch looked at Patch. Hank looked at Fetch. 36

"I think Patch is stronger. He carries heavy loads," said 46
Mitch. He put a large pack on Patch's back. 55

"I think Fetch is stronger," said Hank. He put his own 66
large pack on Fetch's back. 71

Mitch looked at Fetch. Hank looked at Patch. Each man 81
said, "Your mule is strong!" 86

School + Home **Directions** Read "Mules" to your child. Then have your child practice reading the story aloud with you. Make sure your child groups words into phrases and pauses briefly for each comma.

Name ______________________________

Cousins

Zoe and Maya are cousins. Zoe is nine, has brown hair, and lives 13
in California. Maya is ten, has black hair, and lives in Texas. 25
Their dads are brothers. Maya is older, but Zoe is taller. Maya 37
does not mind. She runs faster than Zoe! 45

Zoe and Maya like to visit each other. Zoe comes to Texas every 58
Christmas. They put on plays, sing, and dance for the family. 69
Maya comes to California every summer. They go to Maya's 79
favorite place, the beach. Maya builds huge sand castles, and Zoe 90
swims in the waves. 94

They have such a good time that it is hard to go home. Maya and Zoe 110
say goodbye, knowing that they will visit each other again soon! 121

School + Home **Directions** Read the story to your child. Then ask your child to read the story correctly with appropriate phrasing. Make sure your child pauses briefly at commas.

Name ______________________________

Rummage Sale

"Can we go to the rummage sale?" Daniela asked her mother. She 12
had seen the big tent and the colorful signs in the parking lot at 26
school. 27

"Why do you want to go?" Daniela's mother asked, puzzled. 37

"I don't know," Daniela said, shrugging. "I saw the sale outside 48
the window at school, and it looked like fun." 57

Daniela had never been to a rummage sale before, but a lot 69
of people seemed interested in it. She was excited to see a 81
boy pulling a wagon full of books and board games he had 93
brought out of the tent. 98

"Okay," Daniela's mother said. "Let's go." 104

"Thank you!" Daniela said. She wanted to see if the sale had 116
any books and games that she might like to buy. 126

Directions Tell your child to read the story silently before reading aloud. Then take turns reading "Rummage Sale" aloud with your child, paying special attention to appropriate phrasing. Read the story at least two or three times.

Name ____________________

The Deer

One Saturday, Dan woke up early in the morning. He heard a 12
rustling sound. Dan went to the open window and stared. He saw 24
a young deer chewing on the blackberry bush in his yard. 35

Dan tiptoed outside. When he stepped onto the porch, he frightened 46
the deer. In a flash, it leaped over the fence and through the trees. 60

Dan told his sister, but she didn't believe him. "You saw a shadow," 73
she said. 75

Dan's mother didn't believe him either. "You probably saw the 85
neighbor's dog," his mother said. 90

Early the next morning, Dan left a few carrots in the yard near the 104
bush. Dan watched from the porch, but the deer did not return. 116
"Maybe I didn't see a deer," Dan said to himself. 126

A week later, Dan hid near his kitchen window at sunrise. 137
Suddenly, he saw a wonderful sight! 143

In the backyard, the young deer stood with its mother. It lifted its 156
head. Then both deer leaped across the yard and were gone. 167

School + Home **Directions** Read the story to your child, modeling appropriate phrasing. Then have your child practice reading the story to you. Remind your child to pause for commas and to group phrases rather than reading word by word.

Name ____________________

Soccer Rules!

To enjoy soccer, you should know how the game is played. The object of 14
a match or game is for one team to score a point by passing the ball and 31
shooting it across the other team's goal line. 39

Soccer is played on a field with a goal at each end. The match is played 55
in two parts. Players use their feet to kick the ball. They also use their head 71
or chest to pass or block the ball. Except for goalkeepers, players should 84
not touch the ball with their arms, even by accident. Goalkeepers can use 97
their whole body to keep the ball from crossing the goal line. They wear 111
gloves on their hands. 115

Defenders protect the field near goals and try to pass the ball to 128
midfielders. Midfielders cover the middle of the field and might try to 140
score. Or, they might pass the ball to a forward. Forwards should shoot 153
the ball into the other team's goal. When they do, they score! 165

Directions Have your child read the passage "Soccer Rules!" aloud to you. Encourage your child to group words and to pause when he or she comes to a comma. Then take turns reading the passage aloud to each other.

Name ____________________

The New Student

"Students, we have a new student today," Miss Lee said. "His name 12
is Abdi. His family just moved here. Abdi is from Somalia. Can you 25
tell me where Somalia is?" 30

No one answered. The students stared at Abdi. He smiled at them. Then 43
he raised his hand. "Somalia is in Africa," he said, pointing to a map. 57

"Would you please show us, Abdi?" asked Miss Lee, smiling. Abdi 68
walked to the map. He pointed to a country in Africa. 79

"Thank you, Abdi," Miss Lee said. 85

"What is Somalia like?" Dave asked. 91

"Somalia is a little like this country. It has big cities, valleys, and 104
mountains," Abdi replied. "Somalia has hot deserts too!" 112

"What games do people play?" Tina asked. 119

Students began talking all at once. "What foods do you like?" "Do they 132
all talk like you?" 136

Abdi smiled. He looked at the students. They would be his new friends. 149
Abdi was happy. "Maybe they will learn as much from me as I will 163
learn from them," he thought. 168

Directions Read the story aloud with your child two or three times. Encourage your child to pause briefly for commas and to group words together so they make sense. Then ask your child to read the story alone, using appropriate phrasing.

Name ____________________

Annie's New Uniform

Annie put on a red shirt. It had a blue bear on it. Above the bear was 17
her team's name, River Park Bears. She liked the soccer team's new 29
uniforms. 30

First, she looked in the mirror. Then she turned around to show her 43
cat. The big orange cat looked out the window instead. "I like this 56
shirt!" Annie said. Her old uniform was too small. This one was a 69
little big. 71

Then she put on special leg pads. She pulled long red socks over 84
them. "These pads will keep my legs from getting hurt," Annie 95
told her cat. 98

Annie had new shoes too. They had blue stars on them. Annie put on 112
her shoes. She paraded around the room, doing little kicks. "I like 124
these!" Annie said. "I hope we win today." 132

Then she left the house. Annie raced to the park, where her team 145
waited. 146

"Line up!" called the coach. He had a new uniform too! 157

The team did practice kicks. They ran around. They were ready, and 169
they looked great. Annie felt great too. The Bears would win! 180

Directions Read "Annie's New Uniform" to your child. Then have your child practice reading the story aloud with you with appropriate phrasing and pausing briefly for each comma.

Name ____

Jasmine Changes Her Mind

Jasmine was a very stubborn, grumpy girl. Last August, her mother 11
announced, "Jasmine, you're going to visit Grandma and Grandpa on 21
their horse farm." 24

"I'll be bored and lonely!" whined Jasmine. "I might get bitten by 36
a rattlesnake! I'm not going, and I'm not going to change my mind!" 49
Jasmine warned angrily. 52

Jasmine's mother said firmly, "Honey, please go pack because I'm driving 63
you there tomorrow." 66

Jasmine's grandparents lived in an old farmhouse outside the city. They 77
raised and trained horses. Jasmine often made excuses that kept her from 89
visiting her grandparents. She didn't care to visit the farmhouse or see 101
any horses. 103

The morning after Jasmine arrived, Grandma took her to the horse stable. 115
"Jasmine, I'd like to introduce you to Canary," said Grandma. "She's a 127
very calm and gentle horse." 132

"*Canary* is a silly name for a horse," Jasmine said with a frown. "I don't 147
like horses, Grandma, and I'm not going to change my mind!" Jasmine 159
insisted. 160

"I know you don't like horses, honey, but I think Canary might like you," 174
said Grandma. 176

Grandma took Jasmine's hand and placed it against the end of Canary's 188
nose. "It feels like velvet!" Jasmine exclaimed. Then Canary stepped 198
forward, pushing her nose gently against Jasmine's shoulder. "Well, I 208
might like horses a little," Jasmine whispered, smiling at Canary. 218

Directions Read "Jasmine Changes Her Mind" aloud with your child two or three times. Encourage your child to read with correct phrasing by grouping words so they make sense.

Name ____

The Silent Storyteller

Anita's mother, Mrs. Ortiz, uses sign language. Sign language is a 11
special way to communicate using your hands. People who are deaf use 23
sign language to communicate. They make letters and symbols using 33
the movements and positions of their hands and arms. 42

Every Friday afternoon, Mrs. Ortiz goes downtown to the public library 53
to tell stories. Some of the people who come to story time can hear, and 68
others cannot. As a librarian reads stories aloud, Mrs. Ortiz tells the 80
stories in sign language so everyone can enjoy them. She sits on a high 94
stool at the front of the room where everyone can see her as she signs. 109

Anita loves to go with her mother to story time at the library. Anita can 124
hear perfectly well, but she still enjoys watching her mother tell the 136
stories in sign language. Her mother's hands seem to leap and dance 148
in the air as she moves them, as if she were conducting a silent, 162
invisible orchestra. 164

Anita has been learning sign language since she was a baby. Her mother 177
started teaching her signs like "more" and "milk" when Anita was only 189
seven months old. Anita could use sign language even before she 200
could talk! 202

Anita is proud of her mother and the beautiful way she uses her 215
hands to sign. Anita hopes to someday become a silent 225
storyteller just like her mother. 230

Directions Tell your child to read the passage silently before reading aloud. Then take turns reading "Silent Storyteller" aloud with your child, emphasizing appropriate phrasing. Read the story at least two or three times.

Name ____________________

The Water Park

"I'm going on the water slide first!" Akira said. He was walking through 13
the parking lot of the water park. His mother and his brother Kano 26
walked behind him. Akira wanted to get inside the park as quickly as he 40
could. It closed in five hours, and there was so much to do! 53

"I'm going in the wave pool first!" Kano said, skipping. He was happy. He 67
wore his new green swim trunks and flip flops, and he carried a big beach 82
towel. 83

"Boys, you need to stick together. I can't watch both of you if you're in 98
different places at the same time. You will have to compromise," their 110
mother said. 112

Akira thought for a minute. Then he said, "Kano, you're right. We should 125
go to the wave pool first. It makes me feel sick if I go in it after I eat." 144

Kano grinned and started skipping toward the entrance again. "Thank 154
you, Akira. That was very nice of you," Mom said. 164

Akira shrugged. Now he could probably spend the whole afternoon on 175
the water slides. This was perfect. The three of them finally reached the 188
entrance. Mom paid, and they walked over to the wave pool. Mom sat 201
down on a chair, and Akira kicked off his shoes. The boys dropped their 215
towels and ran toward the wave pool. "Be careful!" Mom called. 226

Akira and Kano splashed out into the waves. The sun was hot, the water 240
was cool, and this was going to be a great day! 251

School + Home

Directions Read the story to your child at a natural pace with appropriate phrasing. Then ask your child to read it aloud. Remind your child to pause briefly for commas and to group words together instead of reading word by word.

Name ______________________

Victor and Alma Go Exploring

Victor dreamed of one day becoming a famous explorer. Until then, he 12
would use his imagination. He read every book and watched every movie 24
he could find about adventures. He planned where he would go when he 37
grew up. 39

At home, Victor pretended to be in faraway places, hunting for treasure. 51
Really, he was in his own yard. Victor crept through the bushes by the 65
porch as if they were dark jungles. He walked through the fish pond by 79
the fence as if it were a swamp filled with hungry crocodiles. He even 93
climbed his mother's rock garden. He pretended it was a chain of ragged 106
mountains as he searched the rocks for strange things. Victor found many 118
treasures. He found beautiful rocks. Once he even found a jar of pennies 131
that looked like buried treasure. 136

"Can I help? I want to look too!" Victor's little sister Alma often begged 150
to help. 152

Most days Victor found a way to get rid of his sister, but today he gave in. 169
"Yes, Alma. You can help," Victor said with a sigh. Soon Victor and Alma 183
were deep in the bushes by the porch, searching under rocks and logs. 196

Suddenly Alma pointed and called out, "What's that shiny thing?" 206

Victor sat down by where Alma was pointing. "It looks like a metal box!" 220
Victor said. He dug lumps of dirt from around the box and wiggled it free. 235
He tried to open it, but the box was rusted shut. "You discovered this box 250
all by yourself, Alma. You should come exploring with me every day! But 263
right now, let's show this box to Mom." 271

Directions Read the story together with your child. Then ask your child to read the story aloud with appropriate phrasing by grouping words into phrases that make sense.

Name ____________________

The Clever Squirrel

Each morning, the squirrel looked for food. He found fruit in the 12
forest. He packed away the food in his nest. He needed to save 25
food for the long winter! 30

The other animals were not so prepared. They played away the 41
summer days. 43

Every evening the squirrel returned home to sleep. 51

When winter came, the squirrel had enough food. The other 61
animals were hungry! They had not saved enough food, so they 72
asked the squirrel for help. The squirrel had enough food to share 84
with the other animals. 88

School + Home **Directions** Read the story aloud to your child. Read with feeling to bring the story alive. Then have your child read the story aloud with expression and without making any mistakes.

Name ______________________________

Not Quite Ready

Ray had a big brother named Jake. One day, Jake took Ray 12
to the water park. 16

Jake ran to the pool and jumped in. Ray took a look. He almost 30
jumped in, but he did not. He was not quite ready. 41

Jake climbed up the tall water slide. Then he slid into the cool water. 55
Ray took a look. He almost climbed up, but he was not quite ready. 69

The boys ran to a table. Jake took an apple from his bag. He took 84
a big bite. Ray looked at the apples in his bag. His stomach growled. 98
He was ready! He took an apple and a big bite too! 110

School + Home **Directions** Read "Not Quite Ready" aloud to your child, showing feeling in your voice. Then have your child practice reading the story aloud with you with expression.

Name ____________________

The Move

Billy's family was moving. "We need a bigger house," his mother said. 12

"But I don't want to move!" Billy said. He liked his house just as it was. 28
He didn't want to leave his friend James, and he didn't want to go to 43
another school. His family moved anyway. 49

Then Billy saw his new school and his new house. The school had a huge 64
playground, and his new house had a big park right down the street. 77
Yet Billy still missed his friends, especially James. 85

One day he noticed a boy playing in the yard next door. Billy walked over 100
and started playing with the boy. "I have a new friend already!" he told 114
his mother after she called him home for dinner. 123

Billy still missed James. "I know what I'll do!" thought Billy. "I'll invite 136
James to play with us. We'll all have fun together!" 146

School + Home **Directions** Read "The Move" to your child with feeling in your voice. Then have your child read the story aloud with expression and without making any mistakes.

Name ____________________

Harry Says He's Sorry

Theo and Harry sat at Theo's dining table doing their homework. 11
"Do you want a snack?" Theo asked. 18

"Sure, that sounds great," Harry replied. Theo got up and went into 30
the kitchen. 32

Harry took a break and raised his arms behind his head to stretch. His 46
elbow bumped against a bookshelf behind the table. Harry heard some 57
books fall, and then he heard a loud crash. 66

Harry turned around and saw that he had knocked over a glass dog. He 80
felt terrible! He picked up the pieces and carried them into the kitchen to 94
Theo's mother. "I'm so sorry. I accidentally broke this little dog," he said, 107
showing her the pieces. 111

Theo's mother took the pieces from Harry. "It's okay, Harry. Thank 122
you for being honest," she said. 128

School + Home **Directions** First, have your child read the story silently. Then take turns reading "Harry Says He's Sorry" aloud with your child with expression. Read the story at least two or three times.

Name ______________________________

A Rainbow at Night

Last summer, Alisa visited her friend Tara. Tara's family lived in a 12
large city by the lake. "We'll be busy for the whole week!" 24
Tara promised. 26

After Alisa arrived, Tara taped up a large city map in her 38
bedroom. Tara pointed to different places on the map. "We'll 48
explore special sights around the city!" Terra said. 56

That afternoon Tara's mother took the girls to visit a sidewalk art 68
fair. Alisa stared at a painting of the city's skyline at night. 80

"I call this painting *Rainbow at Night,*" said the artist. "At night, 92
the water near the shore looks like a rainbow of lights." 103

"It's beautiful! I think this is my favorite painting," Alisa said to 115
the artist. 117

"What else would you like to do this week, Alisa?" Tara's mother 129
asked as they left the art fair. 136

"Could we take a boat ride out on the lake some evening?" 148
asked Alisa. "Then I could see the rainbow at night for myself!" 160

School + Home

Directions Read the story aloud to your child. Then ask your child to practice reading the story to you with expression, particularly when reading dialogue. Challenge your child to read without making any mistakes.

Name ____________________

Looking at the Moon and Stars

Jamal pulled on his warm jacket and tied his shoes. He hurried out 13
the door. It was getting late. 19

Jamal's grandfather was already out in the backyard setting up a 30
big telescope. "Tonight we will look at the Moon and stars," said 42
Grandpa. 43

Jamal loved gazing at the night sky. He liked the stories Grandpa 55
told. "When I was a boy," Grandpa said, "my uncle told me 67
the moon was made of cheese!" 73

Jamal chuckled. "Did you believe it, Grandpa?" he asked. 82

"Oh, yes!" Grandpa laughed. "I wondered how that great big ball 93
of cheese got way out there in space. Now I know the moon is 107
made of rock. There are giant holes called *craters* on the moon. 119
Some people think the craters look like a face. Do you see the 132
face?" Grandpa said, pointing at the full moon. 140

Jamal studied the moon. Finally he said, "I see two eyes, a nose, 153
and a mouth." 156

Grandpa smiled. "That's the Man in the Moon." 164

Directions Have your child read "Looking at the Moon and Stars" aloud with you with expression. Practice reading the dialogue in the story with your child, and adjust your voices for each character. Then take turns reading the parts of Grandpa and Jamal.

Name ____________________

The Dog Wash

The students in Mrs. Green's class needed to raise money for a class 13
trip. Students in the class called out ideas, and Mrs. Green took notes. 26

"How about a bake sale?" called Heather. 33

"Maybe a car wash?" asked Andy. 39

"Or dog walking?" said Tameka. 44

"Let's put Andy's and Tameka's ideas together. We can have a DOG 56
wash!" yelled Elisa. 59

Mrs. Green's students thought that a dog wash sounded like fun. 70
They could wash dogs in the school parking lot. The students made 82
signs and put them up. 87

The morning of the dog wash came. Mrs. Green's students were 98
excited. Many people and dogs walked to the school. The dog 109
wash started. The students washed, and the dogs splashed. All 119
the people laughed. 122

Some of the dogs did not like it! They shook their wet coats. The 136
students got wet, but it was still fun. 144

Soon Mrs. Green's students had washed every dog. Then Mrs. Green 155
counted the money they had raised. They had more than enough for 167
the trip! 169

Directions Read the story to your child. Then ask your child to read it with intonation, adjusting pitch and volume to reflect the emotion and meaning of the text. Challenge your child to read without making mistakes.

Name ____________________

The Search

"Have you seen Tiger?" Luis asked. He looked around the kitchen. 11
Luis's cat Tiger always slept in his basket near the table. 22

Yet Luis had not seen the big orange cat all day. 33

"Have you looked upstairs?" Aunt Rosa asked. She stirred a pot on 45
the stove. 47

"He's not there," Luis said. "I'm getting worried." 55

Luis decided to look for Tiger outside. He stepped out into the cold 68
night. "Tiger?" Luis called. He looked under bushes in the dark yard. 80
Where was Tiger? 83

Luis pushed open the door to the big old garage. He had always been 97
afraid of the garage. It was full of boxes. There were many dark 110
corners. Luis always imagined something jumping out at him from 120
the shadows. 122

"Tiger, are you in here?" Luis whispered. His voice sounded small and 134
afraid. "Come on, Tiger. Let's go inside," Luis said. He walked around 146
a pile of boxes. 150

Then something jumped out of the dark and landed on Luis's back. 162
"HELP!" Luis screamed. He reached up. There was something soft and 173
warm on his shoulder. 177

"Tiger, it's you!" Luis cried. 182

Directions Read the story to your child. Ask your child to read the story, using intonation when reading dialogue and sentences ending in exclamation or question marks.

Name ______________________________

Police Horse

Spree works for the police department in Portland, Maine. Spree is a police 13
horse, and Officer Lisa Allen is Spree's human partner. 22

On most workdays, Officer Lisa spends about two hours preparing Spree 33
for work. First, Officer Lisa sprays Spree down, feeds him, and rakes out 46
his stall. Then she puts on Spree's harness, gives him a good combing, 59
and saddles him up. Finally, Officer Lisa puts on her own uniform. Now 72
they're ready to ride the streets of Portland! 80

Spree and Officer Lisa perform serious work. Once they saw a shoplifter 92
running out of a store. They chased him down a street that was being 106
fixed. A police car couldn't have driven around the trucks and workers 118
there, but Spree could! Spree and Officer Lisa caught the shoplifter. 129

Speeding cars, noisy people, and honking horns could spook, or startle, 140
a horse. They're all part of life in the city. How did Spree learn not to be 157
startled? By going to school, Spree learned about city life. He had to get 171
used to the noises of the city and prove he could stay calm. 184

Spree's work is not all serious. Part of his job is to make friends for the 200
police. That's easy! Just seeing him makes people smile. 209

School + Home **Directions** Take turns reading the passage aloud with your child two or three times, with appropriate intonation. Encourage your child to adjust his or her pitch and volume to reflect the meaning of the passage. Challenge your child to read without mistakes.

Name ______________________________

Do Not Open Until June!

"This week, we will make a time trunk," Mrs. Park announced to the class. 14
"Does anyone know what a time trunk might be?" 23

"A time machine?" Joe asked hopefully. 29

Mrs. Park smiled and said, "Not a time *machine,* a time *trunk*. Our time 43
trunk will be like a treasure chest to open at the end of the school year. We 60
will create a collection of objects to remind us what happened in our class 74
and in the news this week. We can put in almost anything!" 86

"We should put in a newspaper and a news magazine," suggested Dean. 98
"A school newspaper too!" added Maria. 104

"Would you like to include drawings and schoolwork?" asked Mrs. Park 115
as she started a list on the board. "Use your imaginations and enjoy 128
yourselves! At the end of the week, you will write labels describing the 141
objects you have chosen. We'll attach the labels and package everything in 153
a cardboard box. Before we seal it with tape, I'll take a photograph of the 168
class to put in the box. Imagine how different you might look when the 182
school year is over!" 186

"How will we remember *not* to open the time trunk?" asked Tony. 198

Mrs. Park thought a moment and said, "Let's write 'DO NOT OPEN 210
UNTIL JUNE!' in capital letters across the front! That should do it!" 222

Directions Read "Do Not Open Until June!" aloud to your child with appropriate intonation. Then ask your child to read the story aloud using intonation. Challenge your child to read the whole story once through without making a mistake.

Name ______________________________

The Faces on the Mountain

You may have visited Mount Rushmore, where the faces of four 11
presidents are carved into a mountain. Mount Rushmore honors these 21
men as symbols of our nation. George Washington stands for the fight 33
for freedom from England. Thomas Jefferson stands for government by 43
the people. Abraham Lincoln brought the states back together. Theodore 53
Roosevelt was chosen for his work with governments around the world. 64

Work was begun in 1927 under the direction of artist Gutzon Borglum. He 77
chose the southeast side of the mountain because it received good sun for 90
most of the day. "Here is the place!" Borglum decided. 100

Before Borglum could begin, the hard surface of the mountain had to be 113
blasted away. Borglum stated, "American history shall march along that 123
skyline!" 124

Soon Borglum and his men began carving the presidents' faces with 135
special drills and blades. They used a small model as their guide. Much of 149
the carving was done as they hung in harnesses attached to strong ropes. 162
The ropes were hooked into the cliff above. It was dangerous work, but 175
not one man lost his life. 181

Washington's face was carved first. Washington's face was revealed on 191
July 4, 1934. Before the ceremony, a 70-foot-long flag covered the carving. 203
Next, workers began Jefferson. After two years, the stone was found to be 216
badly cracked. Jefferson was blasted away and started again. Work 226
continued until 1941, the year that Gutzon Borglum died. 235

Since then, visitors to Mount Rushmore have looked in wonder at the 247
faces of four men who helped shape American history. 256

School + Home **Directions** Take turns reading the passage with your child, using appropriate intonation. Then ask your child to read the story aloud without making any mistakes.

Name ______________________________

The View Through Blanca's Camera

Everywhere Blanca went, she kept her camera close. She hung it on a strap 14
around her neck or stuffed it into her pocket or backpack. Blanca often 27
took pictures of common things that appeared boring but looked interesting 38
and different when the pictures were printed. 45

One day, Blanca had an idea for some new photographs. At dinner, she 58
said, "Papi, I would like to take some pictures, but I will need your help! 73
May I please come to work with you on Saturday?" Blanca's father was a 87
construction engineer. Blanca knew all about the machines that he used. 98

Papi said, "Let's see what Mami says. I think it will be all right. What 113
pictures are you planning to take?" 119

"The giant crane!" said Blanca. Her eyes widened. She was so excited. 131

"What's so special about the crane?" asked Papi. He was puzzled. The 143
crane was useful, but it did not seem very interesting. 153

"It's not special until I take the picture," Blanca told him. "Before I aim 167
my camera, I will decide where to stand so it looks just right. I will move 183
around until I get enough light, so the picture will not come out dark. The 198
crane will be moving, but in the picture it will be still," she said. 212

"Oh, Blanca, you cannot stand near the crane when the arm swings. It is 226
too dangerous!" Papi said. 230

Blanca thought about that for a minute. "That's okay, Papi. The arm does 243
not have to move. The big crane will look so cool against the blue sky! Oh, 259
Papi, I can't wait!" 263

School + Home

Directions Take turns reading the story aloud with your child. Encourage your child to adjust his or her intonation, especially when reading dialogue. Challenge your child to read the entire story without mistakes.

Name ______________________________

Too Hot!

"Mom, it is too hot!" Adam said. It was too hot to play baseball. 14

Mom was in the kitchen. She was making dinner. "You could 25
cut up some carrots," she said. 31

"I want to go outside, but it is too hot!" Adam said again. 44

Mom thought for a moment. "Why not water the lawn? You 55
could get out the sprinkler. Then you could run through the 66
water. That might cool you down," she said. 74

"That is a great idea!" said Adam. 81

School + Home **Directions** Read the story to your child, giving each character a distinct voice. Then take turns reading aloud with your child. Read the passage three or four times, and check that your child adjusts his or her voice to reflect each character.

Name ______________________________

Class Trip

Mrs. Davis asked the class for ideas for their class trip. 11

"Let's go to the zoo!" Michael said. 18

"No, let's go to the beach!" Sara said. 26

All the kids started talking at once. "Students, one at a time!" 38
Mrs. Davis said. 41

Jason raised his hand. "Can we go to the park?" he asked. 53

"These are all good ideas," Mrs. Davis said. 61

Molly raised her hand. "I want to go to the museum," 72
she said. 74

Other kids nodded. "That sounds cool!" Sara said. 82

"We will go to the museum," Mrs. Davis said. 91

School + Home **Directions** Read the story to your child. Model reading with expression, and adjust your voice for each character. Then ask your child to read the story aloud with appropriate expression and characterization.

Name ______________________________

A Fancy Dinner

"Follow me," the waiter said. Stacy walked behind her mother and 11
older sister Kerry. Their grandmother followed Stacy. 18

Stacy hurried to sit next to Grandma Kay. Today was a very special day. 32
All the girls got together each year for dinner to celebrate Mother's Day. 45

This year Grandma Kay picked a fancy restaurant. Stacy looked at 56
the menu. She wasn't sure what she wanted to eat. She wasn't sure 69
what some of the food was! 75

"I think you'd like this," Grandma Kay said quietly, pointing at a 87
spot on the menu. 91

Stacy read it out loud. "Steak with pommes frites and seasonal 102
fruit." 103

"Pommes frites are French fries," Grandma Kay said. 111

"Oh, that sounds delicious!" said Stacy. 117

School + Home **Directions** Read the story to your child. Model reading with expression, and adjust your voice to reflect each character when reading dialogue. Then have your child practice reading the story to you in the same way.

Name ______________________________

The Car Show

Tim's dad was always busy. Yet he promised to take Tim to the car show 15
on Saturday. 17

That week Tim's dad worked late. "Where's Dad?" Tim asked his mother 29
one night. 31

"He's still at work," she said. "It's a busy week." Tim worried that his dad 46
might not have time for the car show. 54

On Saturday, Tim's dad ate breakfast and read the paper. Then he took 67
Tim's sister Emma to the store. After he got back, he helped a neighbor fix 82
his lawn mower in the garage. It was getting late. "Did Dad forget about the 97
car show?" Tim asked his mom. 103

Just then Tim's dad came in and washed his hands. "Well, Tim, you better 117
hurry up and get changed if we're going to make it to the car show!" he 133
said, eyes twinkling. 136

School + Home **Directions** Read the story aloud to your child, modeling reading with expression and characterization. Then have your child practice reading the story aloud in the same way.

Name ______________________________

The Lost Dog

Juan stroked the big dog's thick yellow fur. The dog wagged its tail and 14
looked up at Juan. It seemed to be smiling. 23

"He's wearing a collar, but there's no tag on it," Juan's mom said. 36
"His owner must miss him." 41

That afternoon Juan and his mom made "Found Dog" signs. They posted 53
the signs all over the neighborhood. 59

Secretly, Juan hoped no one would come looking for the dog. He really 72
wanted to keep him. 76

Then the phone rang. The signs had worked. 84

Soon the dog's family came to get him. "Petey!" the children cried, hugging 97
the big dog. The dog jumped up, licked them, and wagged his tail. 110

"Thank you for taking care of Petey," a tall, smiling man said to Juan. 124

Sadly, Juan watched the family drive away. "You were very responsible 135
with that dog," Juan's mom said. "Would you like a dog of your own?" 149

"Oh, yes!" Juan shouted joyfully. He couldn't wait to get a dog. 161

Directions Read the story aloud to your child, modeling how to adjust your voice to reflect each character and his or her mood and feelings. Then ask your child to read the story aloud, using different voices for Juan and Mom. Remind your child to think about what the characters might be feeling and how they might sound.

Name ____

Sports Day

Anthony could not wait for Sports Day. Students at Anthony's school would 12
sign up to play their favorite sport for the coming year. Anthony wanted to 26
sign up for soccer. 30

The morning of Sports Day, Anthony leaped out of bed excitedly. Then 42
he stopped. His throat was sore. He felt hot, and his whole body ached. 56
Anthony's mom looked worried. "You do not look well. Let's take your 68
temperature." 69

Soon Anthony was back in bed. "You are staying home from school today," 82
his mom said. "I will call the doctor." 90

"Oh, Mom," Anthony said. "Today is Sports Day!" 98

Anthony stayed in bed for three days. When he finally went back to school, 112
sports sign-up was over. Most of the sports were full. 122

"There's one spot open in tennis," the gym teacher said. 132

Anthony rolled his eyes, but tennis was his only choice. 142

The following week, Anthony went to tennis practice. The more he played, 154
the more he enjoyed tennis. Soon Anthony had a new favorite sport. 166

Directions Have your child read "Sports Day" aloud to you. Encourage your child to read with characterization and expression, adjusting his or her voice when reading dialogue for Anthony, his mom, and the gym teacher.

Name ______________________________

Ethan Makes a Choice

It was the Fourth of July. Ethan and his family were packing a picnic 14
dinner. All of their neighbors were going to the park to see fireworks. 27
Ethan heard that this year's show would be amazing. 36

"Dad, I know what you said. Could I PLEASE light just ONE 48
firecracker?" Ethan asked. 51

"Ethan, I said no fireworks, and I meant it," Dad replied. 62

"But they are so cool!" Ethan said. 69

"Playing with firecrackers is dangerous. You could get hurt," 78
Dad told him. "I don't want to see you near any fireworks." 90

That evening Ethan helped clean up after dinner. As he cleaned up 102
the yard, he saw something in the grass. A firecracker! 112

Ethan looked around. He saw his family waiting for the fireworks. No 124
one was looking at him. He picked up the firecracker. Then Ethan 136
stopped. He remembered his dad's words. 142

"Dad!" Ethan yelled. He ran back to his family. "I found this on the 156
ground. I think you had better take it." Ethan's dad smiled at his son. 170

Directions Model reading the story to your child expressively, using different voices for Ethan and his dad. Then ask your child to read the story aloud two or three times with expression. Challenge your child to read the story without making any mistakes.

Name ____________________

New School

Jordan took a deep breath. He pushed open the door and walked 12
into the classroom. The teacher turned and smiled at him. All the 24
kids stopped talking and stared. "Hello," Jordan said. 32

"Good morning, Jordan," the teacher said. "I am Miss Hill." She 43
turned back to the kids. "This is Jordan. He has just moved here. 56
Let's make him feel at home." 62

Eliza raised her hand. "You can sit next to me," she said. Eliza 75
pointed to the empty desk next to her. 83

"Thank you," Jordan said. He sat down and opened the desk. 94
Jordan put away his paper and pens. 101

"Eliza, will you help Jordan follow along today?" Miss Hill 111
asked. She brought Jordan his new books. "We will start our day 123
with writing." 125

Miss Hill went back to her desk. "Take out a pen and paper. Let's 139
write for ten minutes," she said. 145

Jordan took out his pen and paper. What would he write about? 157
"So far, I like my new school. It's not as scary as I thought it 172
would be," he wrote. It was a good day. Jordan was excited to 185
make new friends. 188

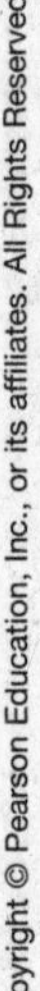

Directions Read the story aloud with your child two or three times with expression. Encourage your child to use different voices for each character's words, showing how the characters are feeling.

Name ______________________________

A New Book and a New Friend

Carrie raced her bike toward the library. She shouted loudly as she rode, 13
"It's here, it's here, it's HERE!" The newest Mystery Mel book, *The Ancient* 26
Treasure, had just come out. Carrie wanted to borrow one of the library's 39
copies. She chained her bike outside and ran up the steps. 50

Carrie searched the new books section and found ONE remaining copy! 61
She hurried to check out the book. On her way, Carrie passed a table and 76
saw her neighbor Lewis glance up at her. 84

"Hey, Carrie!" Lewis said. Carrie was impatient to get home and start 96
reading, so she didn't stop. 101

Suddenly Carrie remembered that she also needed an insect book for 112
school. She set her Mystery Mel book on a windowsill and went to find 126
the insect book. When she returned, her book was gone! Then Carrie 138
noticed Lewis standing at the counter holding it. 146

"You stole my book!" Carrie whispered. 152

"I saw you put it down. I thought someone might take it. Here, I saved it 168
for you." Lewis handed Carrie the book. 175

Now Carrie felt sorry. "Oh. Thanks, Lewis." she said. 184

"I've read all the Mystery Mel books too," Lewis said and smiled shyly. 197
"Maybe we could start a Mystery Mel book club." 206

"I'd like that!" said Carrie. She couldn't wait to talk about the new book 220
with Lewis. 222

Directions Read the story aloud with your child two or three times, emphasizing expression. Encourage your child to use different voices for Carrie and Lewis and to adjust his or her voice to show how the characters are feeling.

Name ______________________________

Chinese New Year

Chinese New Year was only a week away, and May was very happy. “Mother 14
said we can stay up late to go to the parade!” she excitedly told her little 30
sister Ping. Usually, May and Ping had to be in bed by nine o’clock, but the 46
New Year Parade was a very special occasion. 54

In the days before Chinese New Year, May and Ping helped their mother 67
make Chinese dumplings. Mrs. Choi showed the girls how to roll the dough 80
into small circles and carefully spoon in meat and vegetables. The sisters 92
took turns pinching the dumplings closed. 98

Finally, the day of the big parade came! The Choi family watched the 111
amazing show of colorful paper dragons and parade floats from their street 123
corner. Ping was afraid of some of the angry-looking dragons, so she stood 136
behind May and held onto her big sister’s hand. “They’re scary!” Ping 148
wailed. 149

“It’s okay, Ping,” May whispered. “Those are just dancers holding up big 161
paper costumes that *look* like dragons. See their feet underneath? It’s the 173
people dancing that makes the dragons move.” 180

Ping peeked out from behind May. She smiled when she saw the dancing 193
feet under the dragons, but she still held tightly to her big sister’s hand. 207

School + Home **Directions** Read “Chinese New Year” aloud with your child two or three times. Model how to use volume and tone of voice to show fear, excitement, and encouragement. Then ask your child to read the story aloud, using a different voice for each character.

Name ______________________________

Grandpa's Tall Tale

One evening during winter vacation, Noah and his older sister were drinking 12
hot chocolate by the fireplace at their grandparents' mountain cabin. Very 23
quietly, Grandpa said, "Did I ever tell you kids about the time I almost 37
caught an alligator?" 40

"Oh, not *that* tall tale again!" cried Grandma. Grandpa loved to tell stories, 53
and this one was his favorite. He told it every time Noah and his sister 68
visited. 69

"Yes, tell us that one again!" Noah cheered. 77

"It was winter," Grandpa began as he touched his chin. "I was riding 90
my horse Bart in Nonsense Canyon when I heard a scratching sound!" 102

Noah's older sister Rachel rolled her eyes and laughed. "*Nonsense* is right, 114
Grandpa! Alligators do NOT live in the mountains." 122

Grandpa talked in a hushed and excited voice. "Yes, that scratching was 134
the sound of an alligator dragging its rough-skinned tail in my direction! 146
I whirled Bart around with a jerk, and there stood the alligator! He stared 160
down at me with those narrow eyes, his hungry jaws ready to turn me into 175
a juicy meal!" 178

"Grandpa, alligators crawl on their bellies," Rachel said. "They do NOT 189
stand." 190

"How tall was he, Grandpa?" Noah asked, giggling. 198

"That huge beast had to measure fifteen feet tall!" yelled Grandpa. 209

Grandma shook her head, smiling. "The last time, that huge beast was 221
twelve feet tall! He gets taller each time you tell that story!" 233

"That's why it's called a TALL tale!" laughed Grandpa as he slapped 245
his knee. 247

Directions Read "Grandpa's Tall Tale" aloud with your child two or three times using a different voice for each character in the story. Then have your child read the story aloud on his or her own, using expression and characterization.

Name ______________________________

Clean Up!

"This house is a mess!" Mom said. She looked around. There were toys, 13
shoes, and books on the floor. Dirty dishes covered the table. Sam and 26
Angelo were sitting in the living room. They were playing video games. 38

"Boys, turn off that game. We are going to clean up this house," Mom 52
said. She stood between the boys and the television. 61

Sam moved over so he could see around her. "Mom, we're busy! I'm 74
just about to beat this level!" he complained. 82

"No, you're not. You are going to help me, Sam," Mom said with a 96
frown. She turned off the television. 102

"Mom!" Angelo yelled. "Why did you do that?" 110

"Angelo, this house is messy. I did not make this mess by myself," 123
Mom said. 125

"Sorry, Mom," Angelo mumbled. Sam was still mad. He was quiet. 136

Mom sighed. "Let's make this fun. If you bring me the dishes, I will wash 151
them. Let's see if you boys can clean up the living room and playroom in 166
30 minutes. If you do, there will be a fun surprise," she promised. 179

Sam looked up. "What kind of surprise?" he asked. 188

Mom laughed. "If I tell you, it won't be a surprise!" she said. 201

The boys got up and went into the kitchen. They brought their dishes 214
to the sink. As she washed the dishes, the boys picked up their other 228
things. When the 30 minutes ended, the house was clean! 238

"Okay, boys, get your swimming suits. We are going to the pool!" 250
Mom said. 252

Directions Read the story to your child, adjusting the volume and pitch of your voice to reflect the feelings and voice of each character. Then ask your child to use different voices for each character as he or she practices reading the story aloud.

Name ______________________________

Berry Picking

Brendan loves fruit. He likes to pick his own blueberries. Blueberries grow 12
on bushes. 14

First, Brendan gets a basket for his fruit. Then he walks down the rows of 29
green bushes. They are covered with blueberries! 36

Brendan picks lots of blueberries. He puts most of them in his basket. 49
Some he puts right into his mouth! They are very sweet. 60

Soon Brendan's hands are the color blue. His basket is almost full. He will 74
need another basket! 77

School + Home **Directions** Model reading "Berry Picking" aloud with accuracy, with expression, and at a natural rate. Then have your child practice reading the story in the same way.

Name ____

Train Ride

Enrique was excited. He was going to see a ball game. It was his 14
birthday present. He and his parents were taking the train there! 25

They waited at the station. After a few minutes, Enrique heard 36
a train horn. He could see the train's light down the tracks. 48
"It's coming!" Enrique yelled. 52

The train pulled into the station, and Enrique and his parents 63
got on board. Enrique sat by the window. He watched the 74
towns and fields go by as the train rushed to the game. 86

Directions Read the story to your child with accuracy, with expression, and at a natural rate. Then ask your child to read it and match your rate and expression without making any mistakes.

Name ____

The Big Shot!

Shelby dribbled the ball slowly up the court. There were 20 seconds 12
left in the big game, and the score was tied. 22

The referee whistled. "Time out!" he yelled. 29

Shelby picked up the ball and walked over to her team's bench. All of 43
her teammates huddled around their coach. Coach told them the plan. 54

They ran back onto the court. Anne passed the ball in to Shelby. She 68
dribbled around for a few seconds, waiting for Carly to drop into the far 82
corner of the court. 86

Shelby quickly passed Carly the ball. Carly cut along the baseline and 98
put up a shot. The ball bounced off the rim, but Anne was there. She 113
tipped the ball in, and the buzzer sounded. 121

The game was over. They had won! 128

School + Home **Directions** Read "The Big Shot!" to your child with expression and at a natural rate. Then have your child practice reading it aloud with expression, with accuracy, and at a rate that is neither too slow nor too fast.

Name ______________________________

Best Friends

Curt and Luke are best friends. They used to live next door to each 14
other. They were born three days apart in the same hospital! They 26
both have annoying little sisters. Now Curt lives across town, but 37
they play on the same football and baseball teams. 46

Sometimes after practice, Curt sleeps over at Luke's house. They 56
ride bikes around the neighborhood. They help make tacos or burgers 67
for dinner. Those are their favorite foods! Then they watch movies or 79
play games. They always try to stay up late, but Luke's mom makes 92
them go to sleep. 96

When they grow up, Curt and Luke want to go to college together. 109
They will be roommates! Curt wants to be a doctor, and Luke wants 122
to be an engineer. 126

Directions Read "Best Friends" aloud to your child. As you read, model correct intonation by allowing your voice to rise and fall naturally and by emphasizing important words. Then ask your child to read the story in the same way without mistakes.

Name ____________________

Robots

Would you like a machine to clean your room? Would you like a 13
machine to bring you food or play a game with you? Machines that 26
do these things are called *robots*. 32

Robots have a computer inside them. The computer tells them what 43
to do. They will do a job over and over until a person tells them to 59
stop. 60

They do many things. Some mow lawns or help build cars. They can 73
carry heavy things and go into dangerous places. Some walk and talk. 85
Yet they cannot feel happy or sad. 92

Robots go where it is not safe for people to go. They go into space. 107
They do not need air, food, or sleep. They gather information and send 120
it back to Earth. They can go to the bottom of the ocean. They can go 136
into a volcano. 139

Robots are very helpful machines. What do you think about robots? 150

School + Home **Directions** Read the passage to your child. Model reading at a natural rate with expression. Then have your child practice reading the passage aloud with accuracy, with expression, and at a natural rate.

Name ____________________

A Class Garden

Today, Tasha's teacher, Mrs. King, is teaching a lesson. She is 11
showing her class how to grow a vegetable garden. The students 22
will grow different plants in a corner of their classroom. 32

"What have we learned about plants?" Mrs. King asks. 41

"Plants need sunlight, soil, and water," explains Tasha. "Plants 50
also need enough room for their roots to grow." 59

Mrs. King holds up a small jar and measures soil into it. Next, she 73
puts a pea seed into the soil. "Soon a plant will grow in the loose 88
soil. What will happen first?" Mrs. King asks. 96

"A plant shoot will poke out of the soil," says Ellen. "A shoot is a 111
young plant." 113

The students put their jars on a bench against a sunny window. 125
"Keep your plants watered, and they will grow well," says Mrs. King. 137

A week later, Tasha and Ellen check their plants. "Do you see that 150
shoot growing in my jar?" asks Tasha. 157

"I can't wait until my plant grows!" says Ellen. 166

Directions Read the story "A Class Garden" to your child, using your voice to show expression and intonation. Then ask your child to practice reading it to you with accuracy and appropriate expression and intonation.

Name ______________________________

The Queen Who Wished for Gold

Long ago, a silly queen made a wish. “I wish for gold at my 14
fingertips!” she exclaimed. 17

The queen reached for an apple to eat. The fruit turned into gold! 30
Next, the queen reached for a glass of warm milk, but the milk 43
became gold too. “I cannot eat and drink gold food,” the queen 55
cried, “but it will make me rich!” 62

She raced through the castle. She touched everything in sight. Then 73
she touched the people. She even touched her dog! Soon the queen 85
was alone. Her gold dog stared at her. 93

In the garden, she picked a gold flower. “I cannot sniff a gold 106
flower,” the queen said. She dropped it to the ground. 116

That night the castle was quiet. The queen slept on a hard gold 129
bed. She cried gold tears. “I do not want any more gold,” she said. 143
“I wish it would go away.” 149

In the morning, everything had changed back! The queen was so 160
happy. She would never wish for gold again! 168

School + Home **Directions** Read the story to your child. Model reading with expression, especially when reading the queen’s dialogue. Then have your child practice reading the story to you in the same way. Ask him or her to adjust his or her voice when reading the queen’s words.

Name ____________________

Miguel's Pen Pal

"Miguel, can you get the mail?" Mom asked. 8

"Yes, Mom," Miguel said. He opened the door and walked outside. It 20
was a nice day. Maybe he would ride his bicycle with friends. 32

Miguel went to the mailbox and opened it. There were a few letters for his 47
Mom and Dad. There was also one for Miguel! Miguel looked at the letter. 61
It was from his pen pal, Cesar. Cesar lived in Mexico. They met two years 76
ago when Miguel visited his grandparents. Cesar lived on their street. 87

Miguel took the mail inside. He gave his mom her mail. Then he sat down 102
to read his letter. Cesar and Miguel wrote letters every month. This letter 115
was short. 117

"Miguel, I have great news!" Miguel read. "I am coming to visit. Your 130
grandparents are coming too. We will be there next month. I can't 142
wait! We will have fun! See you soon. Cesar." 151

Miguel was so happy. "Mom, Cesar is coming to visit with Grandma 163
and Grandpa!" he yelled. 167

Directions Read the story to your child at a natural rate. Model reading with expression, showing Miguel's feelings as you read his dialogue. Then ask your child to read the story aloud at a regular rate with appropriate expression and without making any mistakes.

Name ______________________________

Isabel's Allowance

Isabel took the clean dishes out of the dishwasher and put them away. Now 14
she just had to clean her room, and she would be finished with chores. Then 29
she could collect her allowance! 34

Isabel raced back down the stairs after cleaning her room and ran into the 48
garage where her father was working. "All the chores are finished!" she 60
gasped. "I'm ready for my allowance now!" 67

"All right, all right," said her father. He brushed off his hands. "What's the 81
big rush?" 83

"I've been saving for three weeks, and now I finally have enough money 96
to buy the new video game I want!" 104

Isabel's father frowned. "That silly game?" he asked. "Isn't that a waste of 117
money?" 118

"What do you mean?" asked Isabel. "Everyone has that game!" she 129
insisted. 130

Isabel's father sighed and handed her the allowance money. "Well, it's 141
your money. You can decide how to spend it, but you might want to save 156
some of it for something important." 162

"Oh, Dad!" Isabel sighed as she ran out the door. 172

Twenty minutes later, Isabel stared at the video game display at the store. 185
"I *thought* I had enough money," she said sadly. The price of the game had 200
almost doubled during the past month. 206

Isabel decided to save her allowance until she could afford the game. Yet 219
two weeks later, she wasn't interested in the game anymore. Isabel was glad 232
she had saved her money. 237

Directions Read "Isabel's Allowance" to your child. Then have him or her read the story with you two or three more times. Encourage your child to use his or her voice expressively when reading dialogue and to group words into meaningful phrases instead of reading word by word.

Name ____________________

The Envelope, Please

Have you ever watched a television show where someone says, "The 11
envelope, please"? Envelopes are made out of paper and are used to 23
hold other papers, but they can also be used to hold things like pictures 37
and money. 39

Before people used computers, people kept in touch by sending letters 50
through the mail. Letters were sealed inside of envelopes both to protect 62
them and to keep them private. 68

Today, most people write letters using computer e-mail. Most of us don't 80
send many letters through the mail anymore, but we can see tiny pictures 93
or icons of envelopes on our computer screens. Envelope icons show 104
where a computer's e-mail tools are. Sometimes an envelope icon will 115
pop up to show that a new e-mail message has arrived. 126

Have you ever written a letter and sent it to someone through the mail? 140
Most people enjoy getting letters by mail. You can even send artwork 152
or photographs inside the envelope with your letter. Photos and drawings 163
make letters more special and fun to read. 171

Try writing a letter to someone you love. Be sure to include the correct 185
address and a stamp on the envelope. Your letter will bring a smile 198
to someone's face, and you just might get a letter in return! 210

Directions Read "The Envelope, Please" to your child. Then ask your child to read the passage aloud with appropriate intonation and expression. Challenge him or her to read without mistakes.

Name ________________________________

The Champion Driver

The big race is about to begin! "Drivers, start your engines!" the announcer 13
calls out. Kim revs the engine. The car rumbles around her. Then the green 27
flag is out, and the race is on! 35

The tires of Kim's race car scream and spin. The car shoots forward with 49
amazing speed! Holding the powerful car steady, Kim drives down the 60
center lane. Going into the first turn, Kim brakes, steers tightly to the inside 74
lane, and pulls ahead. 78

The race fans go wild, and their cheers echo around the track! "Number 91
17, driven by Kim Young, takes the lead! Look at the way she 104
handles those turns!" the announcer yells. 110

It's the last lap of the race. Kim's car screams around the last turn and 125
bounces over the curb. She feels the car start to slip and pulls the steering 140
wheel back to keep the car under control. She really wants to win! Kim 154
speeds ahead, refusing to hit the brakes. As she passes under the 166
checkered flag, the crowd leaps up to cheer their new champion! 177

"Kim, are you daydreaming again?" The voice of Kim's English teacher 188
interrupts the cheers. 191

Kim sits up quickly. "I'm sorry, Mr. Stewart," she says. Kim feels bad. She 205
should pay attention in class. Kim just really likes racing. 215

"You should be writing a report about your dream job," Mr. Stewart 227
tells her. 229

"Yes, sir," Kim says, smiling. "I already know what I am going to write!" 243

Directions Read the story aloud to your child. Then ask your child to read the story with expression and at a natural rate. Challenge him or her to read the whole story once without making any mistakes.

Name ______________________________

Band Class

"What instrument are you going to play?" Monica asked. She and her friend 13
Alicia walked down the hall toward the band room. It was their first day in 28
band class, and neither girl knew what to expect. 37

"I am not sure yet. Maybe flute or clarinet," Alicia said. "My mom told me 52
that I'm not allowed to play the tuba." 60

Monica laughed. "Tuba? You could not even hold up a tuba. It would not 74
even fit on the bus!" she said. She laughed again, picturing tiny Alicia 87
carrying a big tuba onto the bus. "My mom told me I'm not allowed to 102
play the drums," she added. "She said that the neighbors would be angry." 115

Alicia laughed. "I think we can find something else to play," she said. 128

The girls walked into the band room and took seats on the floor. The bell 143
rang. The band director, Mr. Rivera, stood at the front of the room. "Let's 157
get started. Do any of you already play an instrument?" he asked. 169

Several students raised their hands. "I play piano," Ann said. Mr. Rivera 181
listened as each student told him what he or she played. He wrote a list 196
on the board. A few people already played instruments in the band. 208

"This is a good start. Next, each of you will choose an instrument to try. 223
There is no pressure. If you don't like it after two weeks, you can try 238
something new," Mr. Rivera said. 243

Monica leaned over toward Alicia. "I think I will try the trumpet," she 256
whispered. "It looks like fun." 261

"Cool!" Alicia replied. 264

Directions Read "Band Class" to your child. Then ask your child to practice reading the story aloud with appropriate expression and intonation. Check that he or she reads accurately and at a natural rate.

Name ____________________

Wesley's Cast

Wesley's right arm hurt. It also itched! Wesley had a green cast 12
on his arm. 15

"Nice cast! What happened?" Wesley's friend Eric asked. 23

"I fell off my bike," Wesley told him. "I got a big scratch on 37
my leg too." 40

"Can I sign your cast?" Eric asked, pulling a pen out of 52
his bag. 54

Wesley nodded. "Sure!" Wesley held out his arm and Eric 64
signed the cast. "Cool! Thanks!" Wesley said. Maybe all of 74
his friends would sign it too! 80

School + Home **Directions** Have your child practice reading "Wesley's Cast" to you until he or she can read it without making any mistakes. Challenge your child to read with appropriate phrasing and expression.

Name ______________________________

Fresh Paint

Juan looked around his room. It looked like a room for a two-year-old! 13
Little blue trains lined the walls. His mother had painted the trains 25
before Juan was born. It was embarrassing. 32

“Can we paint my room?” Juan asked his mother. “Please!” 42

“I like your room. What’s wrong with it?” his mother asked. 53

“Those little blue trains are kind of young,” said Juan, rolling his eyes. 66

“Well, what do you want it to look like?” his mother asked. 78

“Blue and orange!” said Juan. His baseball team’s colors were blue 89
and orange. 91

Juan’s mother thought a moment. “All right, let’s paint!” she said. 102

Directions Read the story to your child at a natural rate. Model reading with feeling, such as showing excitement when you read a sentence with an exclamation mark. Then ask your child to read the story aloud with feeling and at an appropriate rate. Challenge him or her to read without making any mistakes.

Name ______________________________

The Big Storm

BOOM! Rob woke up when the thunder rumbled outside his 10
window. He looked over at his alarm clock. It was 2:30 in the morning, 24
still too early to get up. 30

Lightning flashed, lighting up the room for a second. BOOM! 40
BOOM! The thunder was getting louder. 46

Suddenly Rob's door opened. His little brother, Danny, poked 55
his head into the room. "Rob, can I come in? It's really scary 68
in my room," Danny said. 73

"Sure, Danny. Come on in," said Rob. Danny carried in his pillow 85
and blanket. He spread them out on Rob's floor and closed the door. 98

Just then, something howled outside of Rob's door. "What was that?" 109
cried Danny. 111

Rob opened the door. It was just their dog, Fred. He was more afraid of 126
storms than anyone! 129

School + Home

Directions Read "The Big Storm" to your child. Model reading with appropriate expression and intonation and reading each word correctly. Then ask your child to read it to you without making any mistakes. Remind him or her to say words in all capital letters louder than other words.

Name ______________________________

Meteor Shower

"When will it start, Grandpa? I'm bored!" Maddie complained. She 10
was sitting on the hood of her grandfather's car, and she was freezing. 23
They were parked in a field far from town. It was very dark. 36

Grandpa was setting up his telescope nearby. "Very soon, Maddie. 46
You have to be patient. This only happens a few times each year," 59
he said. 61

Maddie sighed. She was cold and tired. It was hours later than when 74
she normally went to bed. 79

Maddie looked up. There were more stars than usual up there. Then 91
one of the stars streaked across the sky. Then another and another! 103
"Grandpa! It's starting! The meteor shower is starting!" she cried. 113

She and Grandpa watched as meteors flew across the sky. It 124
was worth the wait! 128

Directions Read "Meteor Shower" to your child. Model adjusting your voice to read with feeling and give each character a distinct voice. Then ask your child to read the story in the same way. Challenge him or her to read without mistakes.

Name ______________________________

Street Fair

"It's eight o'clock!" yelled Mom. "Time to go to the street fair." 12
Mom, Dad, Sarah, and Ron walked to the park. Their dog, Buff, went 25
with them. First, they watched a puppet show. Then Sarah and Ron 37
watched a clown do tricks. Next, they watched a bike race. Sarah and 50
Ron cheered for their neighbor who was in the race. 60

At twelve o'clock, they ate lunch in the grass. Of course, Buff was 73
hungry, too. Dad gave him a ham sandwich. Then the family sat and rested. 87

At two o'clock, Sarah entered Buff in a pet contest. Ron went to play 101
a ball game. Buff got a ribbon, and Ron's team won. Dad gave Buff 115
another ham sandwich. He bought Ron and Sarah ice cream. 125

At five o'clock, the family had a picnic in the park. They listened to a 140
band and danced until the sun went down. Even Buff danced. At nine 153
o'clock, they went home. Ron and Sarah hoped there was a street fair 166
the next weekend, too. 170

School + Home **Directions** Model reading the story with expression and at a natural rate. Then have your child practice reading the story. Remind him or her to group words into phrases that make sense.

Name ______________________________

Snowman

When Noelle woke up, snow was falling outside her window. She 11
ran to her door and poked her head out into the hall. "Mom!" 24
Noelle called. "It's snowing!" 28

From downstairs, Mom called back, "I know! Come down and 38
have some breakfast. Then you can go outside." 46

Noelle got dressed and hurried down to the kitchen. She could 57
smell pancakes and bacon cooking. There was a big plate of 68
food waiting for her. "Thank you!" she said, smiling. 77

Noelle ate quickly. She couldn't wait to go out in the snow. It 90
was the first big snow of the winter, and she could tell there were 104
at least five inches on the ground. 111

"I'm going to make a snowman!" Noelle said. She put on her coat, 124
hat, and gloves. 127

Noelle went out into the yard. She rolled three balls: a small one, 140
a medium one, and a big one. She put the two smaller balls on 154
top of the bigger one. She added a carrot nose, some coal for eyes 168
and a mouth, a scarf, and a hat. The snowman was done! 180

Directions Read "Snowman" to your child. Model reading at a natural rate with appropriate phrasing and expression. Then ask your child to read the story aloud in the same way. Challenge him or her to read without making any mistakes.

Name ____________________

The Monster Under the Bed

"Sara, I'm scared!" Anna said. She pushed open the door and 11
walked into Sara's room. Anna was Sara's little sister. 20

Sara sat up in bed and looked at the clock. It was very late and 35
very dark. She yawned. "Anna, go back to bed," Sara said. 46

"No! There is a monster under my bed. It keeps making noises," 58
Anna said. She walked over to Sara's bed and sat down. 69

Sara yawned again. "Let's go look," she said. Sara got out of bed. 82
She took Anna's hand, and they went to Anna's room. 92

Sara heard a scratching noise. It was definitely under Anna's bed. 103
Sara got down on the floor and looked under the bed. All she 116
could see was a shape moving in the dark. 125

"What is it?" Anna cried. She stood near the door. 135

"I don't know," Sara said. "It is too dark." She looked around 147
the room. There was a flashlight on the desk. Sara took it and 160
turned it on. She got down on the floor again. 170

When she shined the light under the bed, Sara laughed. She saw 182
their cat chasing a rubber band. "It's just the cat!" she said. 194

Directions Model reading the story to your child at a regular rate, letting your voice rise and fall naturally. Give each character a different voice, and adjust your voice to reflect the characters' feelings. Then ask your child to read the story without making mistakes and using appropriate expression and intonation.

Name ______________________________

The Lady Next Door

Miss Green lived next door to Kim. Some children in the neighborhood 12
were afraid of her. Once she had yelled at Kim for climbing a tree. “Get 27
out of that tree! You will fall out and break your neck!” After that, Kim 42
stayed away from Miss Green. She had not seen her in months. That was 56
fine with Kim. 59

That summer Miss Green let her flowers grow and grow. Tall plants 71
covered her windows. Kim’s mother was worried. “I think she is getting 83
too old to work around the house,” she said. “Maybe we can help her. 97
Let’s bring her a pie. We can see if she needs help.” 109

Then Kim’s mother got sick. She asked if Kim would take the pie 122
without her. 124

She brought the pie over and asked Miss Green if she needed help 137
around the yard. Miss Green looked worried. “Does my yard look that 149
bad? My son was going to help me, but he’s been so busy.” 162

Miss Green looked outside and said, “Oh, dear! Could you help me cut 175
some plants?” Kim helped her, and then they ate pie. Miss Green said, 188
“Thank you for the help *and* for the company.” 197

Directions Read the story to your child at a natural rate. Model reading with expression, and give each character a distinct voice. Then ask your child to read it aloud, matching your rate and expression without making any mistakes.

Name ______________________________

Do Animals Know?

Is it going to rain? This is a question for a weatherperson, but animals 14
may know the answer too. Watch the animals where you live. They may 27
know more about the weather than you think. 35

Air pressure changes when a storm is coming. Scientists think that this 47
change makes animals behave differently. Before a storm, some animals 57
move around and make a lot of noise. These behaviors may be important 70
warning signals. 72

Many animals get ready for a violent storm by looking for a safe, dry place. 87
They know that some storms are dangerous, and they don't want to get 100
hurt. Bats often screech loudly and fly into buildings before severe weather. 112

Rabbits find hiding places deep in the forest. Butterflies crawl under leaves 124
to protect their wings. These animals are looking for shelter from the 136
powerful winds and heavy rains that storms can bring. 145

If you are on the beach and you see a lot of sea crabs, it may be time to 164
leave. A storm might be coming! Sea crabs don't like strong waves, so they 178
look for shelter on land. 183

If you are planning to do something outside, study the animals near your 196
house first. They may have important news about the weather! 206

School + Home **Directions** Read "Do Animals Know?" with your child. Repeat words or sentences that are difficult for your child. Then ask your child to practice these words or sentences until he or she can read the entire passage fluently and without assistance.

Name ____________________

At Splendid Shore

On August 1st, Beth and her family left for a vacation at Splendid 13
Shore. Beth enjoyed the twists and turns of the highways as they drove to 27
the beach. Beautiful forests, hills, and valleys appeared and then vanished 38
into the distance as the car passed by. 46

When they finally arrived at the beach cottage, Beth hollered happily, 57
"We're here! Come on, everybody, let's go swimming!" 65

"Unpack first!" insisted Beth's mom. 70

After unpacking, Beth and her family changed from their clothes into 81
bathing suits and walked to the beach. The water sparkled in the sunshine. 94
It felt wonderful as it washed over Beth's feet. She and her brother Mark 108
swam in the shallow water. They shrieked with delight as they jumped and 121
splashed in the ocean waves. 126

"Don't go out too far," their father warned. "The ocean currents can be 139
strong and swift!" 142

"OK, Dad, we'll be careful!" Beth called loudly over the roaring sound of 155
the waves. 157

The next moment Beth felt something tangled around her leg. She reached 169
underwater and pulled up a handful of green, slippery grass. "What *is* this 182
stuff?" she asked, wrinkling her nose. 188

"It's just seaweed," Mark laughed. 193

"Yuck!" Beth said as she swam backward, away from the seaweed. "Hey, 205
let's go build a sand castle! Last one up the beach is a bunch of soggy 221
seaweed!" 222

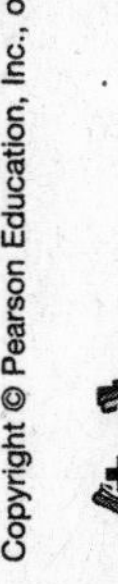

Directions Take turns reading aloud "At Splendid Shore" with your child two or three times. Encourage your child to use his or her voice expressively when reading dialogue and sentences ending in exclamation or question marks.

Name ______________________________

Bad Day

Drew was having a very bad day. First, he spilled juice on his favorite shirt 15
at breakfast. Then he tripped and skinned his knee on his way to school. 29
He wasn't cut, but his pants were torn. When the bell rang, Drew was 43
hoping things would get better. 48

"Okay, students. Pass your homework to the front," his teacher, 58
Mrs. Ross, said. 61

Drew looked through his bag. Where was his homework? He'd worked on it 74
for hours last night. Drew looked again. His whole math folder was missing! 87

Drew raised his hand. "Mrs. Ross, I think I forgot my homework," he said. 101

Mrs. Ross frowned. "Then you will have to take a zero for the work," 115
she said. 117

It wasn't fair! Drew slumped in his chair. This day was just getting worse. 131

At lunch, Drew's banana was squished, and his mother had given him his 144
little brother's egg salad sandwich by mistake. Egg salad made Drew's 155
stomach turn. 157

After lunch, Drew was looking forward to playing soccer with his friends. 169
But as they walked out to the field, it started to rain! After school, Drew's 184
mother had an appointment, so he had to walk home in the rain. 197

By the time Drew got home, he was soaking wet. He really wanted a snack, 212
but there were no more cookies left. Drew's little brother liked to take 225
cookies when no one was looking. 231

When Drew's mother came home with his brother, Drew was in the 243
kitchen, looking for his homework. 248

"I brought you a surprise!" Drew's mother said. She held up a bag. It was 263
Drew's favorite snack, fresh blueberries. His day was finally getting better! 274

Directions Read "Bad Day" to your child, modeling reading with feeling. Then ask your child to practice reading it to you the same way with accuracy and at a natural rate.

Name ______________________________

Trains

A train is a line of cars that move along tracks. Trains have been around 15
for thousands of years. People or horses used to pull the cars. Trains became 29
far more useful when the steam engine was invented in the early 1800s. 42
The steam engine was powered by burning coal. It pulled the cars along 55
the tracks much faster, moving things and people across long distances. 66

Trains changed the world. People and things could cross the United States 78
in a few days. Railroad companies built millions of miles of track. In the 92
1890s, large cities started building train tracks inside cities. These trains 103
would carry people to other places in the city. Today many people still ride 117
trains every day. These trains use electricity or diesel fuel instead of coal. 130

In the United States, people started riding trains less as cars and air travel 144
became cheaper. In the 1930s, the government built millions of miles of 156
highways. People began traveling more by car. In Europe and Asia, more 168
people use trains to go places. 174

The first high-speed train began running in Italy in 1939. The train could 187
go around 125 miles an hour, much faster than cars. The train was even 201
faster than an airplane for short trips. By the 1960s, high-speed train lines 214
were built in Japan, China, and Europe. High-speed trains are also called 226
bullet trains because the front of the trains looks like a bullet. The fastest 240
high-speed trains today go up to 250 miles an hour. They travel along 253
magnetic tracks. People across Europe and Asia ride high-speed trains to 264
go to work and to travel. 270

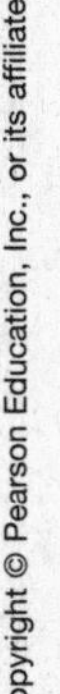

Directions Read the passage to your child at a natural rate. Model reading expressively to make the passage interesting. Then have your child practice reading the passage aloud. Remind him or her to read silently first to become familiar with the words.